Fish & Shellfish

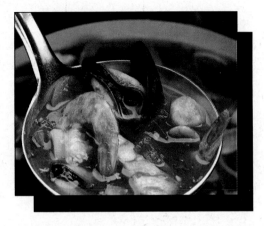

LONNIE GANDARA
Writer

ANNE COOLMAN
JILL FOX
Editors

LINDA HINRICHS
CAROL KRAMER
Designers

JACKSON VEREEN
Photographer

M. SUSAN BROUSSARD
Food Stylist

ALLISON ANTHONY
SUSAN MASSEY WEIL
Photographic Stylists

RIC MYERS
Assistant Photographer

Danielle Walker (*far left*) is chairman of and founder of the California Culinary Academy. **Lonnie Gandara** (*left*), a teacher, lecturer, cook, culinary event organizer, caterer, food consultant, and author, holds an advanced certificate from Le Cordon Bleu in Paris, France. The variety of her food expertise reflects her extensive travel and study in France—she has studied at the Academie du Vin in Paris—Italy, Mexico, and Hong Kong. She is a member of the International Association of Cooking Schools, the American Institute of Wine and Food, and the San Francisco Professional Food Society.

The California Culinary Academy Among the forefront of American institutions leading the culinary renaissance in this country, the California Culinary Academy in San Francisco has gained a reputation as one of the most outstanding professional chef training schools in the world. With a teaching staff recruited from the best restaurants of Western Europe, the California Culinary Academy educates students from around the world in the preparation of classical cuisine. The recipes in this book were created in consultation with the chefs of the California Culinary Academy. For information about the Academy, write the Office of the Dean, California Culinary Academy, 625 Polk Street, San Francisco, CA 94102.

Front Cover

Combine the recipes in this book, your imagination, and seasonally fresh fish and shellfish to create professional-style meals at home. This beautiful salmon steak dish is based on the Grilled Tuna recipe on page 48.

Title Page

Each fish, shellfish, and vegetable brought together in this Seafood Stew (page 34) will maintain its distinct flavor if correctly cooked.

Back Cover

Upper left: Lobster Medallions in Chard (page 27) is an exciting entrée of delicious chunks of steamed lobster meat covered with melted butter.

Upper right: Two trouts garnished with lemon and parsley are ready to enter the fish poacher, where they will be simmered in white wine and herbs.

Lower left: A rich veal stock of leeks, carrots, potatoes, onions, garlic, and herbs can be used in a variety of ways for everything from soup to sauces.

Lower right: Colorful fruits add style to Cold Fillet of Sole With Cilantro, Lime, and Pomegranate (page 20). These poached fillets are folded to create an attractive and appetizing meal for any occasion.

Contributors

Calligrapher
Chuck Wertman

Additional Photographers
Michael Lamotte, back cover: upper right and lower left
Laurie Black, Academy photography
Fischella, photograph of Danielle Walker

Additional Food Stylists
Amy Nathan, back cover: upper right and lower left
Jeff Van Hanswyk, at the Academy

Editorial Staff
Toni Murray
Catherine Pearsall
Rebecca Pepper

Art and Production Staff
Linda Bouchard
Deborah Cowder
Lezlly Freier
Anne Pederson
Raymond F. Quinton

Special Thanks
Acacia Glass; California Crayfish; Ceramic Showcase; Cookin'; Edinburgh Castle; Sue Fisher-King; Barbara Flemming; David Gandara; J. Goldsmith Antiques; Diane Gould; Forrest Jones; Kass Kapsiak; Tom Kaye; Adrianne Kohler; La Mediterranee; Betty Miller; Ric O'Connell; Pasha Restaurant; Ryan's Cafe; Tina Salter; Stonestown Fish and Poultry; and all the cooks and chefs who contributed recipes.

The California Culinary Academy series is produced by the staff of Ortho Information Services.

Publisher
Robert L. Iacopi

Editorial Director
Robert J. Dolezal

Production Director
Ernie S. Tasaki

Series Managing Editor
Sally W. Smith

Systems Manager
Leonard D. Grotta

Photographic Director
Alan Copeland

Address all inquiries to:
Ortho Information Services
575 Market Street
San Francisco, CA 94105

Copyright © 1985
Chevron Chemical Company
All rights reserved under international and Pan-American copyright conventions.

2 3 4 5 6 7 8 9
86 87 88 89 90

ISBN 0-89721-060-3

Library of Congress Catalog Card Number 85-072802

Chevron Chemical Company
575 Market Street, San Francisco, CA 94105

Purchasing & Preparing Fish & Shellfish

The current culinary emphasis is on meals that are light, nutritious, fresh, and easy to prepare. Fish and shellfish fit all these criteria. They also take less time to cook than just about any other type of food, making them perfect for quick family meals or for easy, elegant entertaining. Because of improved transportation, refrigeration, and freezing methods, a wide choice of species is now available across the country. And fish such as trout and catfish are now farm-raised, adding to the range of fresh fish available to the public.

The recipes in this book call for specific cuts of fish. You can purchase whole fish and cut it up yourself, or purchase fish that is cut and ready to cook. There are only two types of whole fish: flat and round, as illustrated by the top two fish in the photograph. Starting below the flatfish and moving clockwise, the most common cuts of fish include: whole pan-dressed fish (a small fish with head and tail, scaled, finned, and gutted); pan-dressed body (without head and tail); steak (a cross-section of fish); butterflied fillet (both sides of the fish still connected); fillets without skin; and fillets with skin.

PURCHASING FISH

The most important factor in choosing a fish is freshness. A truly fresh fish should not smell fishy; a fishy smell is a sign of age or improper handling by the fishmonger. A fresh fish has a mild odor; firm, elastic flesh that springs back when pressed; clear, protruding eyes; reddish or pink gills; and scales that are shiny, bright, and tight to the skin.

When buying steaks or fillets look for flesh with a natural sheen that is free from yellowing or browning around the edges. If the fish has been frozen, ask how long it has been defrosted. Do not buy anything that has been defrosted for more than two days. It is better to purchase frozen fish and defrost them at home. For best quality, try to find fish that were individually quick-frozen on the fishing vessel.

PREPARING FISH

From the structural perspective there are two types of fish: roundfish and flatfish. Both types need to be cleaned before use, but the cleaning procedures vary.

SCALING AND FINNING

Almost all fish require scaling. Some exceptions are trout, whose scales are an integral part of the skin, and catfish, whose tough skin must be removed altogether.

If poaching the whole unboned fish, leave the dorsal and anal fins attached; they will help hold the fish together during poaching.

1. A wet fish is easier to scale; put salt on your hands for a better grip. Remove scales using a knife or scaler. Start at the tail and scrape toward the head. Rinse the fish well.

2. The dorsal fin (pictured here) can be clipped with scissors as shown, although it leaves part of the fin connected to the fish. To remove the whole fin, cut along each side of the fin with a knife and pull the fin toward the head to remove it. Use the same method to remove the anal fin (closest to the tail on the bottom). Clip other fins with scissors.

GUTTING

If you plan to bone and fillet the fish, remove the entrails by gutting through the belly. If serving the fish whole, preserve the shape by gutting through the gills. The gutting techniques for roundfish are different from those used for flatfish.

Roundfish

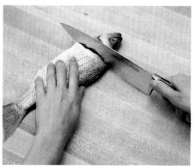

1. Cut off head behind gill opening. Cut open belly from head end to just above anal fin area (see little finger in photo). Remove membranes, blood veins, and viscera. Rinse.

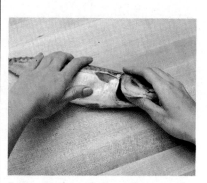

2. To gut through the gills, open the outer gill with your thumb. Reach a finger into the gill and snag the inner gill. Pull gently to remove inner gill and viscera. Rinse.

Flatfish

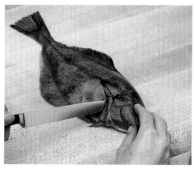

To gut a flatfish, make a small cut behind gills and pull out viscera.

SKINNING

Though many pan-sized fish have tasty skin that enhances flavor, some fish, such as large-mouthed bass and butterfish, have strong-tasting skin, which interferes with the flavor of a dish. Leave skin on when poaching or grilling a whole fish.

Roundfish

1. To skin a whole roundfish, make a slit across the body just behind gills and another slit just above tail. Make another cut down the back.

2. Using a thin knife, separate the skin from the flesh, starting at the tail. Pull (don't saw) the knife toward the head, holding the skin firmly with your other hand.

Flatfish

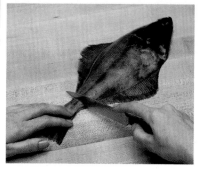

1. To skin a whole flatfish, place the dark side of the fish up, and cut

across the skin where the tail joins the body. Beginning at the cut, peel the skin toward the head until you have formed a flap that you can grasp with one hand. Pull the flap away from the cut while anchoring the fish with your other hand.

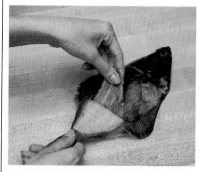

2. Pull the skin over the head. Turn the fish over. Holding the head, pull the skin down to the tail.

Catfish

1. To skin a catfish, cut the skin just behind the head all the way around the body.

2. Wear gloves. Hold head firmly and use pliers to peel skin toward tail.

CUTTING FILLETS AND STEAKS

Fillets are long pieces of boneless fish. Steaks are cross-sections cut from a whole fish. Roundfish and flatfish require slightly different filleting techniques.

Roundfish

1. To fillet a roundfish, make a slit along backbone from head to tail.

2. Next, make a cut behind gill. Holding head, insert knife between fillet and ribs. Sliding knife along ribs, cut down the length of fillet. Pull fillet free and sever skin at the anal fin. Repeat the filleting process on the other side of the fish.

Flatfish

1. Place the skinned flatfish on a board with the eyes up. Cut through the flesh to the backbone (which is in the middle of the fish) from head to tail. Insert the knife blade at a shallow angle between the ribs and the end of the fillet close to the head. Cut down the length of a fillet on one side of the backbone and remove it.

2. Cut the remaining top fillet using the same technique. Turn the fish over. Remove the two bottom fillets.

SKINNING A FILLET

To skin a fillet, place it skin side down and cut a small section of flesh away from the skin close to the tail. Hold knife at a 15-degree angle to the cutting board. Holding skin taut, scrape the knife along the skin without cutting it.

CUTTING A STEAK

Using a large, sharp knife, cut off the head just behind gills. Slice the fish into steaks of the desired thickness, usually between 1 and 1½ inches.

PURCHASING AND PREPARING SHELLFISH

The diversity of shellfish is truly amazing. The major groups are univalves (abalone and conch), bivalves (oysters, clams, and mussels), crustaceans (crabs, shrimp, and lobsters), and cephalopods (squid and octopus). In spite of the diversity, however, all shellfish share one trait that concerns the cook: Once out of the water, shellfish deteriorate quickly and become inedible. Though technology has provided many ways to keep shellfish alive for marketing, some shellfish, such as sea scallops, razor clams, and geoduck clams, are so fragile that they rarely appear alive in markets. These species cannot close their shells completely and die rapidly when removed from their environment. Shellfish of this kind are cleaned, shucked, and refrigerated upon capture.

IDENTIFYING SHELLFISH

The various shellfish pictured at right are: *Top row:* Dungeness crab, purchased live or cooked; spiny lobster, almost always purchased cooked; American lobster, almost always purchased live. *Second row:* crayfish, best purchased live, although they are available frozen; blue (or soft-shell) crab, available live or frozen. *Third row:* oysters, purchased in the shell or shucked; mussels, always purchased in the shell; New Zealand mussels, also always purchased in the shell. *Fourth row:* scallops, usually purchased without the shell, although they are fresher in shell; clams, which can be purchased in the shell or shucked and cooked; shrimp, almost always purchased without heads, and which are almost always frozen at some point in the shipping process. *Bottom:* squid, usually purchased fresh or frozen. Although abalone is not pictured here it is available fresh on the Pacific Coast and frozen or canned in other areas.

This array of shellfish is described in "Identifying Shellfish," at left. Check the "Guidelines" section (page 13) for special purchasing information.

OPENING BIVALVES

Oysters, clams, and mussels should be alive when purchased. The shells will be closed tightly or will snap shut when tapped on the counter. Scrub the shells thoroughly with a stiff brush under cold water. Soft-shell clams are fragile; take care not to break them. Now the bivalves are ready to be opened. Keep in mind that you may substitute cooked mussels in recipes that call for clams.

Oysters

Opening oysters often takes strength. Wear a heavy glove or use a towel to protect your hand from the rough shell. Use an oyster knife with a short, strong blade and hand guard to make the job easier.

1. Wearing work gloves or using a heavy cloth, hold the oyster with the deep cup of the oyster down. Insert the tip of oyster knife into the hinge and twist it to open shell.

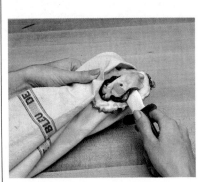

2. Slide knife along inside of upper shell to sever the muscle that attaches it to the flesh. Discard upper shell. Slide knife under flesh to sever bottom muscle.

Clams

A blunt clam knife tip avoids slicing the meat during opening.

1. To open a clam, slide the blade of a clam knife into the seam between the two shells. Work knife between shells toward the hinge until you can pry the shells apart.

2. Slide blade along inside of one shell to sever connecting muscles and under clam to dislodge it from shell. Refrigerate bivalves for a few hours or freeze for 30 minutes to relax muscles; they will be easier to open.

Mussels

To debeard a mussel is to pull out the byssus, the threads of tissue that protrude from the shell. Mussels die soon after debearding, so preparation should follow immediately. Open a mussel as you would a clam.

CLEANING CRABS

The two most common types of crab sold alive are the Dungeness crab and the blue crab. Other types—stone crab from the Southeast and rock crab and Jonah crab from the Atlantic coast—are available live in select markets; Alaskan king crab and snow crab, from colder northern waters, are usually sold frozen, either in sections or as crabmeat.

Hard-Shell Crabs

Wash and scrub hard-shell crabs under cold running water. At this point the entire crab may be either poached or steamed. If, however, you cut up the crab to use in a recipe, you must first kill and disjoint it, then remove the inedible parts as described below.

1. Hold the crab firmly against the work surface. Kill it instantly by stabbing the crab just behind the eyes with the point of a sharp knife. Turn the crab over.

2. Gently fold back the apron or tail flap. Twist and pull off the apron. The intestinal vein is attached and will pull out along with the apron. Discard both. Turn crab right side up.

Hold on to the crab body where the apron was removed with one hand, and use your other hand to pry up and tear off the top shell. Discard the shell.

Soft-Shell Crabs

A soft-shell crab, also known as a buster, is a blue crab that has molted, or shed its shell for a larger one.

Squid

Squid that is tough and unappetizing has been overcooked. Squid can be poached, sautéed, fried, stuffed and baked, or grilled.

3. Remove gills from each side of crab and take out the grayish sand bag. Pull out and discard mandibles from front of crab.

1. Cut across the eyes with kitchen shears or a sharp knife. Reach into the cut and pull out the gray saclike stomach, called the sand bag. Discard the stomach.

1. Rinse squid in cold water. Cut off the tentacles just above eye. Squeeze the thick center part of the tentacles, which pushes out the hard beak. Discard the beak.

4. Holding the body where the legs are attached, apply pressure so that the crab splits in half along the center of the body. Fold back the halves and twist them apart.

2. Turn the crab over, lift up the flap or apron, and fold it down away from the body. Gently pull out the apron and attached intestinal vein. Discard apron and vein.

2. Squeeze the entrails from the body by running your fingers from the closed to the cut end. Pull out the transparent quill that protrudes from the body.

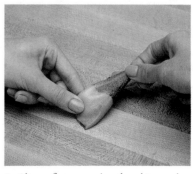

5. Twist off claws and legs where they join the body. Crack them with a nutcracker and remove the meat.

3. Turn crab right side up. Lift flaps at each side near the legs, then scrape off and discard the spongy gills.

3. Slip a finger under the skin and peel it off. Pull off edible fins from either side and skin them.

COOKING LOBSTER

Lobster is sold whole either alive or cooked. When cooked whole they are killed by the heat of the poaching liquid. For recipes that call for raw pieces, you must kill and cut up the lobster, as described below, before cooking.

American Lobster

American lobster has meat in both the claws and body. The flavor of the meat is held in high esteem. The roe and the liver, or tomalley, are also great delicacies. If purchased cooked, make sure the tail is pulled up underneath the body; this is a sign that the lobster was alive when cooked.

1. Hold lobster right side up on a firm surface. With a sharp knife, pierce the shell and flesh at the center of the cross-shaped mark behind the head.

2. Cut in half lengthwise. Remove and discard gravel sac near the head and intestinal vein in the tail. Remove the gray-green tomalley (liver) and any roe from the body and reserve for flavoring sauces.

3. Twist off and save all the claws. Then, with a sharp knife, separate each of the two halves between the tail and the body. (Depending on the recipe, the body may or may not be used.)

4. Slice the tail between every other shell segment, leaving the shell intact. Crack the claws and joints, leaving the shell in place.

Spiny Lobster

This warm-water lobster, also known as rock lobster, has its meat in the tail. The uncooked frozen tails in supermarkets are probably spiny lobster. A smaller variety is marketed as langoustine or rock shrimp. If you are starting with a live spiny lobster, hold it on its back on a firm surface, and with a heavy, sharp knife, stab the point into the mouth to sever the spinal cord. Then turn the lobster over and split in half lengthwise. Use a rubber mallet, if necessary, to force the knife through the body. If you are starting with a cooked spiny lobster, begin preparation by splitting in half.

With both cooked and uncooked lobsters, rinse the viscera from the body and the intestinal vein from the tail under cold running water.

Shrimp

Shrimp are usually sold without heads. If still attached, twist the head off. The entire shrimp body is edible.

1. Remove the legs. Peel a bit of the shell from the head end of the body. Holding the peeled section with one hand, pull the tail with your other hand, and the shell will come off.

2. Slit the shrimp down the outside curve and remove the intestinal vein. On larger-sized shrimp the intestinal vein contains grit that would interfere with the taste of the recipe. Often on medium-sized shrimp no grit is present and the intestinal vein need not be removed before serving.

Crayfish

Crayfish are also called crawfish or crawdads. The meat is in the tail. Crayfish are cooked in their shells. Many cooks devein them. The orange substance in the head and attached to the upper part of the tail of fresh crayfish is a delicious fat. This fat adds richness to crayfish dishes and can often be substituted for butter in a recipe.

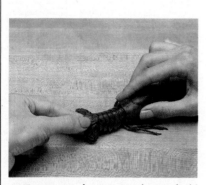

1. To remove the intestinal vein, hold the crayfish securely on a firm surface, right side up. Lift the center tail flap and twist it carefully to free it from the body.

2. Holding the crayfish firmly with one hand, pull the tail flap away from the crayfish to remove the intestinal vein.

GUIDELINES

As with other kinds of foods, each variety of fish has a season in which it is most abundant, least expensive, and at its best. A reputable fish dealer is the best source of information about seasonal buying.

In terms of the character of the flesh, all fish fall into one of two categories: lean or oily.

Leaner fish have a mild flavor and firm white flesh. The oil or fat (5 percent or less of total body substance) is concentrated in the liver. Take care when applying dry-heat cooking processes to lean fish; they dry out easily. Examples of lean fish include sole, flounder, turbot, cod, pollack, sea bass, rockfish, snapper, drum, bass, and burbot.

Oily fish contain 5 percent to 50 percent fat. They usually have flesh that is richer, stronger tasting, and less white than that of lean fish. The fat is distributed throughout the flesh, which helps keep the fish moist during cooking. Examples of oily fish are swordfish, smelt, salmon, bluefish, tuna, mullet, mackerel, trout, catfish, sablefish, sturgeon, and pompano.

Purchasing Tips

When buying fish to be served whole, allow about 1 pound per serving. For fillets and steaks allow 6 to 8 ounces per serving. Remember that half the total weight of a roundfish is head, tail, and bone. About one third the total weight of flatfish is edible.

The flesh of shellfish should be firm and have a sweet smell. An aroma of ammonia in shellfish is a sign of deterioration. Do not store shellfish in fresh water; fresh water will kill them. Shellfish absorb bacteria from polluted water readily, so choosing a reputable dealer is an important step in finding good-quality shellfish. If you plan to catch your own fish or shellfish, always check with local fish and game departments to determine the areas that are safe for harvest. Prepare shellfish soon after capture or purchase.

Cooking Rules of Thumb

When cooking crustaceans in the shells, the color of the shell will change, indicating that cooking is complete. The exception to this rule is lobster; directions for testing lobsters for doneness are on page 18. The shells of bivalves (mussels, clams, scallops, and oysters) will open when they are fully cooked. (Discard any that do not open.) When cooking shellfish out of the shell, note when the flesh becomes firm to the touch; this signals doneness.

With a few exceptions, all fish—whether freshwater or saltwater—can be cooked by following the guidelines presented at the beginning of each chapter. Freshness and a knowledge of the cooking method will assure a successful dish. Each chapter cites the correct cooking method and gives timing guidelines. The primary caveat in fish cookery is: Do not overcook.

A general rule of thumb for frozen fish is not to defrost them completely; thawing breaks down the delicate flesh. Cook frozen fish for almost twice as long as fresh fish.

The Canadian Department of Fisheries has developed this relatively reliable guideline for the timing of fish cookery: Measure the fish at its thickest point; for every inch of thickness allow ten minutes of cooking time.

Although the Canadian method is a good guide, the cook is still the best judge of properly cooked fish. The opacity test is the most reliable way to determine doneness. Use a pointed knife inserted into the thickest part of the fish to check the flesh. Properly cooked fish will be opaque and will not cling to the bones. When using a cooking method that involves intense heat, such as deep-frying, the fish will cook faster than it would if baked in the oven at a moderate temperature. Use the Canadian method to get a rough estimate of cooking time and, as the fish cooks, use the opacity test to tell when the fish is done to perfection.

Lobsters and mussels cook over coals on a bed of stones rounded by the sea. This simple method of cooking shellfish is centuries old.

Poaching, Steaming, Braising & Stewing

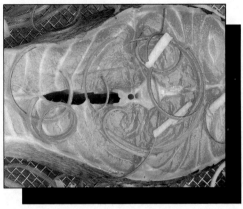

Fish and shellfish are composed of delicate proteins that require delicate cookery; overcooking results in dry, unappetizing fish. Fortunately, moist heat provides a gentle means of cooking that is suitable for any type of fish or shellfish. Moist-heat cooking methods—poaching, steaming, braising, and stewing—use liquid as a cooking medium. The differences among these methods lie in whether the food is cooked above the liquid (steaming) or in it (poaching, braising, and stewing), and in whether the cooking liquid is served as a part of the finished dish (braising and stewing) or not (poaching and steaming).

TIMING

Cooking times for all types of moist-heat cooking can be based on the Canadian Department of Fisheries guideline, explained on page 13. The opacity test, also explained on page 13, is the best way to tell when fish is properly cooked: The fish is done if the flesh is opaque and does not cling to the bones. Remember that internal heat continues to cook a fish after you remove it from the heat source.

POACHING

The two key elements in poaching are the type of liquid used and the temperature of the liquid. Although simple salted water can be used, a more flavorful approach is to use a well-seasoned liquid called *court bouillon.* The temperature of any poaching liquid is critical. The best way to poach delicate proteins like fish and shellfish is to begin with a cold liquid and bring the liquid with the fish in it to a simmer. The proper heat for poaching will barely move the surface of the liquid. This will prevent the outside of the fish from cooking before the inside and helps prevent the fish from falling apart. Also, if a whole fish is placed directly into hot liquid, the skin will split.

When poaching a whole fish, wrap it in cheesecloth first. The cheesecloth preserves the shape of the fish and facilitates removal from the liquid. It does not affect cooking time.

Almost all types of fish are suitable for poaching. The exception is fish with very soft, fatty flesh, such as sablefish or butterfish, which tend to fall apart in the liquid.

Poaching Liquids

The three most widely used poaching liquids are wine court bouillon, vinegar court bouillon, and milk-and-lemon court bouillon. The wine and vinegar court bouillons are flavored with vegetables and herbs. After 30 to 45 minutes of simmering, the mixtures are cooled and are ready for use as a poaching liquid. Vinegar is more acidic than wine and has a more assertive taste, so less of it is needed. The pungent flavor of vinegar works well with fish that have a strong taste, such as mackerel or tuna.

Wine court bouillon is the most common and is an all-purpose bouillon. The strength of a wine-based court bouillon depends on when the cook adds the wine. Adding the wine at the beginning and simmering it evaporates the alcohol, making a mild bouillon. Adding the wine halfway through the cooking time imparts a definite taste of wine.

Milk-and-lemon court bouillon does not require preliminary cooking. It is the most delicate of the court bouillons, and is often used with very mild or white-fleshed fish.

A fish *fumet,* or concentrated fish stock (see recipe on page 17), is richer than court bouillon and will help give more flavor to bland fish. A fumet may be a simple water-based stock made with a few vegetables and fish carcasses, or it may be a wine or vinegar court bouillon enriched with fish trimmings. If court bouillon is destined for a fumet, reduce it to concentrate flavor. In either case fish fumet is imbued with the flavor of fish, making a rich liquid that is often used as a base for sauces to accompany poached fish.

WINE COURT BOUILLON

Both wine and vinegar court bouillon are reusable. Just strain, reboil, and add about 1 cup of water to compensate for the liquid lost in cooking. The bouillons freeze well, too.

> 8 cups cold water
> 4 cups dry white wine
> 2 large onions, peeled and chopped
> 2 carrots, peeled and chopped
> 2 ribs celery, chopped
> Large bouquet garni (see Note)
> 2 tablespoons salt
> ½ teaspoon black peppercorns

1. In a saucepan combine water, wine, onion, carrots, celery, bouquet garni, and salt. Simmer for about 25 minutes. Add peppercorns and simmer for another 10 minutes. (Peppercorns tend to turn the court bouillon bitter if they cook too long.)

2. Let the liquid cool, then strain.

Note A *bouquet garni* is simply a bunch of herbs tied together. If fresh herbs are not available, tie dried herbs in a bag made of cheesecloth. Thyme, parsley, and a bay leaf are the most common constituents of a bouquet garni. Use other herbs for different flavors.

Vinegar Court Bouillon Prepare with the same ingredients as Wine Court Bouillon except use 1 cup red or white wine vinegar in place of the wine. Simmer for about 40 minutes before adding peppercorns, then simmer another 10 minutes. Cool, then strain.

MILK-AND-LEMON COURT BOUILLON

This mild court bouillon requires no preliminary cooking.

8 cups water
½ cup milk
4 teaspoons salt
1 lemon, thinly sliced, seeded

Combine all ingredients. Place fish in liquid and poach.

FISH FUMET
Fish stock

When disassembling the fish carcasses to fit the pot, be sure to remove all skin and gill tissue. Skin imparts a gray color to the stock, and gills impart a bitter taste.

Like bouillons, a fish fumet freezes well. If you refrigerate rather than freeze, however, reboil the stock if it stands for more than three days.

2 pounds fish heads and carcasses, rinsed and broken into pieces
1 large onion, cut in chunks
1 carrot, cut in ½-inch slices
1 rib celery, cut in ½-inch slices
1 bouquet garni (see page 16)
10 cups water
½ teaspoon salt
10 black peppercorns

1. In a large pan place fish trimmings, onion, carrot, celery, bouquet garni, water, and salt. Bring to a boil over low heat, skimming occasionally as scum rises to the surface. Simmer for about 20 minutes.

2. Add peppercorns, then continue to simmer for 10 more minutes. After 30 minutes of cooking, the fish stock is done. Further cooking causes a bitter flavor.

3. Strain the stock through a colander without pressing down on the mass. Pressing the solids clouds the stock, making it unsuitable for an aspic or a clear sauce.

Makes 8 cups.

Poached crayfish in wine court bouillon (see Basic Poached Shellfish recipe, page 18) is a perfect menu for an informal gathering. Guests shell their own crayfish, and the host provides plenty of napkins, cool drinks, and perhaps a variety of sauces to accompany these tasty morsels.

BASIC POACHED SHELLFISH

Poaching is an easy way to cook shellfish—the shells seal in flavors and juices. Use salted water or one of the court bouillons as the poaching liquid. Court bouillon enhances the flavor of the shellfish. Served with any of the sauces beginning on page 114, poached shellfish make a simple, delicious entrée for any luncheon or dinner.

> Lobster or crab or shrimp or crayfish
> Court bouillon (pages 16–17) or salted water to cover

1. Add shellfish to cold poaching liquid, then bring to a simmer. (Many people still plunge lobsters directly into boiling water, but this exposure to high heat toughens them. It is also less humane. The method of slowly heating the water also slowly numbs the lobster. The anesthetized animal expires when the water reaches about 80° F.)

2. Begin calculating cooking time when the fish and liquid reach a simmer. Cook shellfish about 20 minutes per pound.

3. Lobster is done when a small leg can be jerked off easily. (Or insert a rapid-response thermometer into the vent hole at the end of the tail. A 165° F reading means the lobster is fully cooked.) Lobster is not necessarily cooked through when the shells turn red. In contrast, crabs and crayfish are finished when their shells change color. Shrimp are cooked when they change color and become opaque.

ANGLER AND PRAWNS IN CIDER

Angler, often called the poor man's lobster, is also known as monkfish. It is easily substituted for lobster. Conversely, you may use lobster in this recipe. If you do, add the lobster shells to the prawn shells.

> 1 pound angler (monkfish)
> 8 cups Wine Court Bouillon (page 16)
> 1 pound medium prawns, shelled and deveined
> 4 tablespoons unsalted butter
> 1 cup minced onion
> ½ cup minced celery
> ¼ cup minced carrot
> Prawn shells
> 4 cups unpasteurized cider
> 2 tablespoons unsalted butter
> 2 tablespoons flour
> Salt and pepper
> 3 green onions, slivered (4-inch strips) (for garnish)
> ¼ cup minced parsley (for garnish)

1. Remove all membrane from the angler and cut it in 2-inch, diagonal slices. Pour 6 cups of the court bouillon into a large saucepan. Add angler and bring to a simmer. Poach angler for 2 to 3 minutes. Remove from pan and keep warm.

2. Add prawns to court bouillon. Poach 2 to 3 minutes or until barely pink. Remove from pan.

3. In large kettle melt the 4 tablespoons butter. Add onion, celery, and carrot. Cook for 2 minutes. Add prawn shells and stir with a wooden spoon until shells turn pink. (If using lobster instead of angler, break up their shells and cook with prawn shells.) Vegetables should become golden brown.

4. Add cider and remaining 2 cups court bouillon and bring to a simmer. Simmer slowly, uncovered, for about 10 minutes. Strain everything into a saucepan, pressing down with wooden spoon to extract all the juices from the shells and vegetables.

5. Reduce the strained mixture until about 2½ cups of liquid remain.

Knead the 2 tablespoons butter and flour together, then whisk into sauce bit by bit. Allow sauce to thicken.

6. Season with salt and pepper. Return drained prawns to sauce. Place angler on heated platter; pour sauce over all. Garnish with green onions and parsley.

Serves 6.

STURGEON WITH CALVADOS AND APPLES

The use of apples, Calvados, and cream is typical of the cooking style in the regions of Normandy and Brittany. Calvados is the finest of the apple brandies.

> 3 Golden Delicious apples
> 2 cups apple juice
> 2 pounds sturgeon, cut in 6 pieces
> ¾ teaspoon salt
> ½ teaspoon freshly ground pepper
> ½ cup Calvados or apple brandy
> 2 to 3 cups Fish Fumet (page 17)
> 3 tablespoons unsalted butter
> 2 tablespoons minced shallot
> 2 tablespoons flour
> ½ cup Lemon Crème Fraiche (page 119)
> Salt and pepper
> 3 tablespoons minced chives

1. Peel apples. With the small end of a melon baller, make as many balls as possible. In a small saucepan bring apple juice to a simmer. Add apple balls and poach gently until barely soft. Remove apple balls with a slotted spoon and reserve.

2. Over high heat reduce apple juice to about 8 tablespoons. Reserve for use in the sauce.

3. Place sturgeon in a large stainless steel or porcelain skillet that has a tight-fitting cover. Sprinkle fish with the ¾ teaspoon salt and the ½ teaspoon pepper. Pour in Calvados or brandy. Add enough Fish Fumet to completely cover sturgeon.

4. Cover and bring to a simmer. Poach for 8 to 10 minutes depending on thickness of the fish. Remove fish to a heated platter and keep warm.

5. Strain fumet through a fine sieve into a saucepan. Over high heat reduce fumet to about 1½ cups.

6. Wipe out skillet used for poaching fish. To skillet add butter; melt over medium-low heat. Add shallot and cook until it begins to soften. Whisk in flour and continue to whisk and cook for 2 minutes.

7. Add reduced fumet mixture and continue to whisk. Bring to a simmer and cook until thickened (about 2 to 3 minutes). Whisk in 3 tablespoons of the reduced apple juice and the crème fraîche. Season to taste with salt and pepper. Return fish to pan and heat through.

8. In small saucepan heat 4 table-spoons of the reduced apple juice. Add apple balls and reheat gently. Add chives.

9. Serve sturgeon napped with sauce and surrounded by apple balls.

Serves 6.

Angler and Prawns in Cider is an elegant recipe, prepared in the classical style, that is not at all difficult to prepare. It makes use of all the flavor found in seafood shells.

The vibrant colors of red pomegranate seeds and green cilantro and limes are a perfect visual foil for lovely white sole. The pomegranate seeds may be frozen and used throughout the year to add color and crunch to various recipes.

COLD FILLET OF SOLE WITH CILANTRO, LIME, AND POMEGRANATE

This dish makes a wonderfully cool summer lunch or a fine first course to balance a heavy entrée such as lamb.

    8 fillets sole
    1 teaspoon salt
    ½ teaspoon freshly ground
       black pepper
   16 sprigs cilantro
    2 jalapeño or serrano chiles,
       seeded, deveined, and minced
    6 to 8 cups Wine Court Bouillon
       (page 16)
       Cilantro leaves
       Lime juice
    8 thin slices of lime
    ½ cup pomegranate seeds

1. Pat fillets dry. Place outer side of fillet down and sprinkle with salt and pepper. Place 2 sprigs of cilantro and some of the chopped chiles in the center of each fillet. Fold the fillets in thirds and place folded side down in a wide, shallow saucepan.

2. Pour court bouillon over fish. The fish should be completely immersed. Cover and bring to a simmer. Poach 8 to 10 minutes. Remove from heat and cool in poaching liquid. When cool, remove from liquid.

3. To serve, sprinkle fish with the cilantro leaves and fresh lime juice. Top each fillet with a slice of lime and some pomegranate seeds.

Serves 8.

TURBOT WITH GRIBICHE

Turbot is a white-fleshed fish, and the milk-and-lemon bouillon keeps the flesh white. *Gribiche* is a classic egg sauce traditionally served with cold poached fish.

- 6 turbot fillets
  Milk to cover fish
  Slice of lemon
  Salt and freshly ground
  black pepper

Gribiche

- 3 hard-boiled eggs
- 2 teaspoons Dijon mustard
  Salt and freshly ground
  black pepper
- 1 cup oil
- 1 tablespoon minced fresh
  chervil
- 1 tablespoon minced fresh
  tarragon
- 1 tablespoon minced parsley
- 1 tablespoon chopped capers
- 1 tablespoon chopped
  cornichons (tiny sweet-
  sour pickles)

1. Place turbot in wide, shallow saucepan. Cover with milk. Add lemon and season with salt and pepper.

2. Cover pan and bring liquid to a simmer. Poach 8 to 12 minutes, depending on the size of the fish. Remove fillet from pan. Serve warm accompanied with Gribiche.

Serves 6.

Gribiche Crush the 3 egg yolks to form a smooth paste. Add mustard, salt (remember that capers and cornichons can be salty), pepper, and oil, mixing well. Add chervil, tarragon, parsley, capers, and cornichons. Cut egg whites into slivers and add to mixture. Serve over poached turbot.

MACKEREL OR TUNA IN WHITE WINE

This dish is a welcome addition to a buffet table as an alternative to the ubiquitous pickled herring. Serve the mackerel with thinly sliced black bread and the onions used during poaching.

- 2 large onions, sliced
- 4 small mackerel or 4
  pounds tuna
  Salt
- 1½ cups dry white wine
- 1½ cups Fish Fumet (page 17)
- 1 cup dry sherry
  Juice of 1 lemon
- ¼ cup olive oil
- 1 teaspoon black peppercorns
- 6 sprigs fresh thyme or
  1 teaspoon dried
- 3 bay leaves

1. Cover bottom of a wide, shallow saucepan with half of the onion. Arrange fish on top, sprinkle with salt, then cover the fish with the remaining onion. Add wine, Fish Fumet, sherry, lemon juice, olive oil, peppercorns, thyme, and bay leaves.

2. Cover and bring to a simmer. Poach for 10 to 12 minutes, depending on the size of the fish.

3. Remove from heat. Cool in poaching liquid. Remove fish from liquid with slotted spoon. Remove onions and cover fish with them. Refrigerate.

4. Serve the chilled fish with the onions and a sprinkling of fresh lemon juice.

Serves 8.

RED SNAPPER AND CUCUMBERS

The sautéed cucumbers have a delicate taste that complements the gingered fish fillets.

- 4 to 6 cups Fish Fumet
  (page 17)
- ¼ cup sake or dry white wine
- 1 piece of fresh ginger the size
  of a quarter coin
- 1 green onion
- 6 red snapper fillets
- ¾ teaspoon salt
- ½ teaspoon freshly ground
  black pepper
- 2 tablespoons peanut oil
- 1 tablespoon minced peeled
  ginger
- 1 teaspoon salt
- 1 clove garlic, minced
- 3 cups peeled, seeded, julienned
  cucumbers (4-inch strips)
- 1 cup slivered green onion
  (¼-inch strips)
- 1 cup fresh basil leaves, cut
  into long strips
- 2 teaspoons sesame oil
- 1 tablespoon soy sauce
  Pepper to taste

1. In large pan bring Fish Fumet, sake, the piece of ginger, and the whole green onion to a boil. Lower heat and simmer 5 minutes.

2. Sprinkle fillets with the ¾ teaspoon salt and the ½ teaspoon pepper. Fold fillets in half. Place in deep pan just large enough to hold fish. Pour fumet mixture over fillets, cover, and bring to a simmer. Gently poach 4 to 6 minutes. Leave fillets in poaching liquid until ready to use.

3. *For cucumbers:* Heat peanut oil in sauté pan. Add the 1 tablespoon minced ginger, the 1 teaspoon salt, and garlic, and cook for 30 seconds. Add cucumbers and cook for 30 seconds, tossing and coating with oil.

4. Add the 1 cup slivered green onion; toss. Then add basil, and toss to combine. Sprinkle with sesame oil, soy sauce, and pepper to taste.

5. *To serve:* Place drained fillets over bed of cucumbers.

Serves 6.

An easily prepared recipe with a distinctive taste, Shrimp in Beer is perfect for a Sunday afternoon gathering. The secret to the texture is the poaching time—overcooking will make the shrimp tough. The flavor can be varied depending on the type of beer you prefer.

SHRIMP IN BEER

The taste of this dish depends on the beer. An imported dark beer adds a bitterness to the sauce that some find appealing. To achieve a more delicate result use an American beer. Serve with plenty of crusty bread to soak up the sauce.

   2 *pounds shrimp, peeled and deveined*
   2 *to 3 cups beer*
   1 *bay leaf*
   2 *tablespoons butter*
   2 *tablespoons flour*
   1 *cup whipping cream*
    Salt and freshly ground black pepper
  ¼ *teaspoon cayenne pepper*
   2 *tablespoons minced parsley*

1. Place cleaned shrimp in saucepan and just cover with beer. Add bay leaf and bring to a simmer. Cook for 4 to 7 minutes or until shrimp turn pink. Remove shrimp from pan.

2. Over high heat reduce beer until 1 cup liquid remains. In another saucepan melt butter, add flour, and whisk to make a paste. Add beer. Cook and whisk until thick.

3. Add cream. Heat and season with salt, black pepper, and cayenne. Add parsley and return shrimp to sauce. Reheat gently.

Serves 6 to 8.

QUENELLES

This classic mousseline recipe is lighter and more delicate than the flour-based panada originally used for quenelles. Before the advent of the food processor, quenelle-making was a laborious task: The flesh of the fish had to be pounded in a mortar, then sieved to remove connective tissue. With the processor, fish is easy to purée. You still need to sieve it because small amounts of invisible connective tissue may remain in the purée. Keeping the ingredients cold helps them absorb the cream and keeps the quenelles light.

> 1 pound sole or other white, firm-fleshed fish, cut in 1-inch pieces and chilled
> 1 egg
> 1 egg white
> 1 teaspoon salt
> ½ teaspoon white pepper
> 2 cups whipping cream, well chilled
> Boiling stock
> Small oysters, well drained (optional)

1. In a food processor fitted with steel blade, purée the sole. Then push purée through a sieve with a wooden spoon and return sieved purée to processor.

2. Add egg, egg white, salt, and pepper. Purée again. With machine running, slowly pour in cream and process until it is all absorbed into fish mixture. Refrigerate the mousseline until ready for forming.

3. *To form quenelles:* Use 2 tablespoons as a mold to form the chilled mousseline into oval balls. As you work, dip the spoons in hot water often. You can also use a large pastry bag with a plain tip to form quenelles.

4. Place formed quenelles in bottom of a large, well-buttered saucepan. Slowly pour boiling stock into the pan to cover the quenelles. Over low heat poach quenelles until they are firm (12 to 15 minutes).

Serves 6.

Ramekin Method A ramekin saves the cook from having to mold the mousseline and, if you wish, serves as the vehicle for an oyster surprise. The *bain marie* (water bath) is essential for even poaching. Preheat oven to 350° F. Heavily butter six 4-ounce ramekins. Fill halfway full with mousseline. Place small oyster in middle of ramekin. Cover top with remaining mousseline mixture. Place ramekins in baking dish and surround with boiling water. The water should come up almost to the top of the ramekin. Bake until a knife inserted into middle of mousseline comes out clean (15 to 20 minutes).

Serves 6.

SHALLOT–RED PEPPER SAUCE

This flavorful and colorful sauce provides an attractive contrast to the pale quenelle. A food processor makes preparation easy, and a thermos allows you to store the sauce for a short time. If you warm the thermos with hot water before adding the mixture, the sauce will keep for a few hours.

> 3 large shallots, minced
> ¼ cup white wine vinegar
> ¼ cup dry white wine
> 2 red bell peppers, peeled and seeded
> 3 egg yolks
> ½ teaspoon Dijon mustard
> 1 cup unsalted butter, melted and very hot

1. Put shallots, vinegar, and wine in a saucepan. Over high heat reduce the mixture to about 2 tablespoons.

2. Fit food processor with steel blade and purée red peppers. Add reduced shallot mixture, egg yolks, and mustard. Process until smooth. With machine running, add hot butter in a slow, steady stream. An emulsion will form. Serve as soon as possible.

Makes 1½ cups.

PICKLED OYSTERS

Keep these tidbits on hand for unexpected guests.

> 2 quarts oysters (in shells)
> ⅔ cup Champagne wine vinegar
> 2 tablespoons whole allspice
> 1 tablespoon whole cloves
> 2 dried hot red peppers

1. Shuck oysters (see page 10) and save liquor. In a medium saucepan bring oyster liquor to a boil. Skim foam from surface. Lower heat and add oysters. Poach until oysters plump and edges begin to curl. Remove oysters with slotted spoon and place in a large glass container.

2. Strain cooking juices through a colander lined with damp cheesecloth into a medium saucepan. Add vinegar, cloves, and pepper. Simmer for 10 minutes, then cool. Strain the mixture over oysters and refrigerate.

Makes 4 cups.

POACHED OYSTER STEW

This type of stew has been popular since early settlers found vast oyster beds along New England's coast.

> 2 quarts oysters (in shells)
> 2 tablespoons unsalted butter
> 2 tablespoons flour
> 3 cups whipping cream
> 1 cup milk
> ¼ teaspoon ground nutmeg
> 1½ teaspoons kosher salt
> Freshly ground pepper to taste

1. Shuck oysters (page 10) and reserve liquor. In a large saucepan, bring liquor to a boil. Skim foam from surface. Lower heat and add oysters. Poach until oysters plump and edges begin to curl. Remove oysters with slotted spoon. Reserve.

2. Combine butter and flour, mixing well. Add cream and milk to liquor and bring to a boil. Turn heat to medium. Add flour mixture, a bit at a time, whisking after each addition. When sauce has thickened, add nutmeg, salt, pepper, and oysters. Heat.

Serves 8.

STEAMING

Steaming is a time-honored process that the Chinese have raised to a culinary art. For centuries the Chinese have known that steaming brings out the best in the ingredients with the least change in flavor. The circulating steam keeps the food moist and prevents loss of freshness and nutrients. Modern science confirms that steaming does retain nutrients and, since it is more difficult to overcook steamed foods, steaming offers some latitude in cooking time. Finally, because steaming is relatively quick and easy, this age-old technique fits neatly into modern life.

Steam from boiling liquids swirls around food and cooks it with intense, moist heat. Known as direct steaming or wet steaming, this process has only three simple requirements: (1) a cooking vessel with a lid, (2) a small amount of cooking liquid, and (3) a rack to elevate the food above the liquid.

The factors that govern successful steaming are simple. The steam must circulate freely in the steamer. Thus, there should be at least 1 inch of space between the plate holding the fish and the steamer walls. At no time should the liquid touch the steamed fish, and at no time should the liquid boil dry. If you are using stacking steamers, the heat source must be strong enough to circulate the steam through the racks. If, upon removing the lid, it is evident that the steam is not reaching the top rack, use only as many racks as will steam effectively. Keep a pot of boiling water on hand to replenish the steaming water so the steam temperature remains constant.

The basic criteria for cooking times also apply to steaming. Allow 10 minutes of cooking time per inch of thickness of fish; use the opacity test as a final check (see page 13).

STEAMED SALMON STEAKS WITH BLACK BEAN SAUCE

Joyce Jue travels throughout the United States and Far East as a cooking instructor and an organizer of special culinary events and tours. Joyce is also a food writer who develops recipes. In this recipe Joyce uses a common Chinese ingredient, salted fermented black beans. They lend themselves beautifully to braising, stir-frying, and steaming. The beans have an indefinite shelf life when stored in an airtight container.

- 4 salmon steaks, each
  1 inch thick
- 1 teaspoon salt
- 4 green onions, flattened with
  the side of a cleaver and cut
  in 2-inch-long sections
- 4 slices of peeled ginger the size
  of a quarter coin, shredded
- 2 tablespoons salted fermented
  black beans, covered with
  water for 5 minutes,
  rinsed, and drained
- 2 tablespoons soy sauce
- 2 cloves garlic, peeled
  and coarsely chopped
- 1 tablespoon dry sherry or
  dry vermouth
- ½ teaspoon sugar
- 1 teaspoon minced
  peeled ginger
- 4 tablespoons peanut oil
  White pepper to taste
- 2 green onions, shredded
  Cilantro (for garnish)

1. Blot salmon dry and sprinkle with salt. Place half of the 2-inch-long green onion sections and half of the shredded ginger on the bottom of a shallow, heat-resistant plate. Arrange salmon steaks in a single layer on top of ginger and green onions. (Use 2 plates and 2 steamers, stacked, if necessary.) Scatter the remaining green onion sections and ginger over the steaks.

2. Combine beans with soy sauce, garlic, sherry, sugar, and the 1 teaspoon minced ginger. Spread ingredients evenly over fish.

3. Fill a wok with boiling water to 1 inch from the bottom of a bamboo steamer. Bring the water to a boil. Put the plate of fish in the steamer, cover, and place the steamer in the wok. Steam over medium heat for 10 minutes. When done, remove from wok. Uncover steamer, tilting lid away from you.

4. In a small pan heat peanut oil until hot and almost smoking. Meanwhile, sprinkle pepper and shredded green onions over salmon. Carefully pour oil over the entire surface of each steak. The oil should sizzle. Serve hot, garnished with cilantro.

Serves 4 to 8.

STEAMED MUSSELS

A favorite in other countries for years, Americans are beginning to discover the wonderful flavor of fresh mussels. As a result fresh mussels are becoming increasingly available. In this recipe the shells act as the steaming rack. Serve the dish with crusty bread to dip in the broth.

- 3 pounds mussels, washed,
  debearded, and scrubbed
  (see page 10)
- ½ cup water
- ½ cup dry white wine
- ¼ cup minced parsley
- 2 cloves garlic, minced
  Freshly ground black pepper

1. Place mussels in a 4-quart saucepan. Add water, wine, parsley, and garlic. Cover pan and place over high heat. Shake the pan once or twice during cooking.

2. When mussels have opened, they are done. Remove mussels from pan and place in heated bowls. Strain hot broth and pour over mussels.

3. Sprinkle mussels with pepper and serve.

Serves 4.

Steamed Salmon Steaks With Black Bean Sauce features some of the basic ingredients of Chinese cooking, including garlic and fermented black beans.

Elegant Lobster Medallions in Chard may be assembled a few hours ahead. Just before serving, steam the lobster and finish the sauce.

LOBSTER MEDALLIONS IN CHARD

This elegant dish provides a useful lesson in sauce preparation. In this and other recipes, use shells to prepare broth. The use of shells to flavor the sauce is a classic cooking technique.

- 2 lobster tails
- 3 tablespoons unsalted butter
- 1 medium onion, minced
- 1 medium carrot, minced
- 1 rib celery, minced
- 2 cups dry white wine
- 8 large leaves chard
  Salt and freshly ground pepper
- 6 tablespoons unsalted butter

1. Remove meat from lobster tails and cut into 8 medallions. Reserve shells.

2. In saucepan, melt the 3 tablespoons butter. Add onion, carrot, celery, and lobster shells. Push down on shells with wooden spoon. Cook for 10 to 12 minutes. Add wine and bring to a boil. Simmer, covered, for 30 minutes.

3. Strain through a sieve lined with cheesecloth, then squeeze the solids in the cheesecloth to extract all the liquid. Put liquid in a small pan over high heat. Reduce liquid to ⅓ cup.

4. Blanch chard in boiling salted water. Trim away the white part, cut the trimmed white part into slivers, and reserve for garnish.

5. With leaves shiny side down, place a lobster medallion in the center of each leaf. Season well with salt and pepper. Wrap each medallion in the leaf and place seam side down on steamer rack.

6. Pour boiling water into steamer, cover, and steam 10 minutes.

7. While medallions are steaming, whisk the 6 tablespoons butter into hot reduced lobster broth, 1 tablespoon at a time. An emulsion will form. Season with salt and pepper.

8. Remove wrapped medallions from the steamer. Pour seasoned emulsion over the leaves, garnish with slivered chard, and serve.

Serves 2.

STEAMED SHRIMP AND EGGS

This is a wonderful luncheon or brunch dish. If smoked salmon replaces the shrimp, it is suitable for breakfast with toasted bagels and fresh cream cheese.

- 2 tablespoons peanut oil
- ½ pound bay shrimp
- ½ teaspoon minced peeled ginger
- 2 tablespoons minced smoked ham
- 1 tablespoon minced green onion
- 1 tablespoon dry sherry
- 4 large eggs, lightly beaten and seasoned with salt and pepper

1. Grease two 12-ounce heat-resistant glass bowls with the peanut oil.

2. Place shrimp in bowls. Scatter ginger, ham, onion, and sherry over top of shrimp. Pour beaten eggs over mixture.

3. Place bowls on steamer rack over boiling water. Cover and steam until eggs are set (6 to 8 minutes).

Serves 2 to 4.

STEAMED WHOLE FISH, CHINESE STYLE

This presentation of steamed fish is a Chinese classic. The use of more fresh onions and herbs at the finish enhances the dish. Serve with steamed or fried rice.

- 1 whole carp or sea bass
- 2 tablespoons soy sauce
- 2 tablespoons dry sherry
- ¼ cup julienned peeled ginger
- 2 green onions, slivered (4-inch strips; use part of the green)
- 8 sprigs cilantro
  Cilantro (for garnish)
  Green onion, slivered (for garnish)

1. Place fish on plate in steaming rack. (If you do not have a steamer large enough, put the plate on a rack in a turkey roaster.)

2. Sprinkle soy sauce, sherry, ginger, and the 2 slivered green onions over fish. Arrange the 8 sprigs of cilantro on top of fish.

3. Pour boiling water into pan until it comes within 1 inch of fish. Cover and steam about 15 minutes; cooking time depends on the size of the fish.

4. Remove plate from steamer and serve fish directly from plate. Garnish with cilantro and green onion.

Serves 6 to 8.

The recipe for Maryland Crab Stew is easily doubled for serving a group. Blue crabs are used here, but other types of crabs may be substituted.

BRAISES, STEWS, AND SOUPS

The terms *braise*, *stew*, and *soup* usually bring to mind a long cooking process. Braising is generally used for cooking and tenderizing tough but flavorful pieces of meat or poultry, but because fish is a delicate protein that disintegrates if subjected to long cooking, braising takes on a slightly different meaning in fish cookery.

In fish cookery to braise is to cook vegetables, herbs, and fish in liquid in order to mingle their flavors and create a more complex taste. The vegetables, chosen to complement the taste of specific fish or shellfish, are cooked first. The fish or shellfish are added near the end. The delicate flavor of trout or snapper goes well with mild, aromatic vegetables such as celery, carrots, and onions. For strongly flavored fish, such as mackerel, salmon, or bluefish, vegetables with an assertive flavor—garlic, tomatoes, and peppers—are used.

By contrast, fish and vegetables in a stew retain their own distinct flavors; they do not mingle as in a braise. This is accomplished by cooking each ingredient just until done. Because different ingredients take varying amounts of time to cook, they are added in stages. The vegetables requiring a longer cooking time, such as potatoes, go into the pot at the beginning, and fragile vegetables and fish are added near the end.

Soups are much like stews but tend to have a more liquid composition. Because fish yields less gelatin than meat, a fish broth has less body than meat broth. Consequently, fish soup often includes some ingredient to add body to the liquid. In the old days, it was bread. Today, many cooks serve fish soups with fried or baked croutons. Rice may also be used to add body; it is used to thicken gumbo, for instance. And finally, chowders contain potatoes to thicken the broth.

PORTUGUESE FISH STEW

This is a clean-tasting fish stew. The distinct flavors and the herbaceous quality of the kale provide a perfect foil for the fish. The original dish used salted cod instead of fresh fish; in this version the smoked ham supplies the extra flavor.

    3   tablespoons olive oil
    2   pounds cod
    ¼   cup fruity olive oil
    3   pounds new potatoes, cooked,
        peeled, and cut in ½-inch dice
    8   cloves garlic, peeled and
        quartered
    1   pound kale, shredded in
        ¼-inch strips
        Salt and freshly ground black
        pepper
    ¼   pound smoked ham cut in
        slivers
    1   cup dry white wine

1. In a large Dutch oven heat the 3 tablespoons olive oil. Add fish to pan, fry 1 minute on each side, and remove from pan.

2. Add the ¼ cup olive oil to pan. Add potatoes and toss over medium heat until coated. Add garlic and sauté 1 minute. Add kale to pan, turning to coat with oil. Cover and cook until the greens begin to wilt (2 to 3 minutes).

3. Sprinkle potatoes and greens with salt, pepper, and slivered ham. Arrange fish on top and pour in wine. Add enough water to barely reach top of greens.

4. Cover and simmer 25 to 35 minutes, shaking pan occasionally. When potatoes are done, correct seasonings and serve.

Serves 6 to 8.

MARYLAND CRAB STEW

This Chesapeake Bay specialty is a basic, easily made crab stew. It uses blue crab, but you may substitute another variety. Serve it with a soda bread or dark pumpernickel.

     5   slices bacon
    1½   pounds onions, chopped in
         1-inch pieces
     ½   pound carrots, peeled and
         cut in ½-inch pieces
     3   ribs celery, chopped in
         ½-inch pieces
     1   large bell pepper, seeded and
         cut in ½-inch pieces
    1½   pounds tomatoes, peeled, seed-
         ed, and cut in ½-inch pieces
     1   large clove garlic, minced
         Salt and freshly ground
         pepper
    12   cups water
     6   ounces clam juice
     2   medium potatoes, peeled and
         cut in 1-inch dice
     3   tablespoons Worcestershire
         sauce
     1   tablespoon lemon juice
     5   tablespoons Old Bay spice,
         or to taste
    12   blue crabs

1. In a large Dutch oven or kettle, sauté bacon until crisp. Remove bacon and reserve. To bacon fat add onions, carrots, celery, bell pepper, tomatoes, garlic, salt, and pepper. Cook for 10 minutes, stirring occasionally.

2. Add water and clam juice. Simmer 1 to 2 hours. Add potatoes. Simmer 30 minutes.

3. Add Worcestershire, lemon juice, Old Bay spice, and crabs. Cover and simmer 15 minutes. Adjust seasonings and top with crumbled bacon.

Serves 6 to 8.

BRETON FISH STEW

The crustiness of the crackers makes this a great fish hash. Serve it hot or cold. Be sure to include the apples and cornichons; they provide a good contrast.

>   2 *pounds rockfish, haddock, or other white-fleshed fish*
>   12 *pilot crackers or 2 cups oyster crackers*
>   ½ *pound salt pork, cut in small dice*
>   4 *potatoes, peeled, partially cooked, and sliced in ½-inch rounds*
>   1 *teaspoon salt*
>   *Freshly ground black pepper*
>   3 *tablespoons chopped parsley*
>   3 *Golden Delicious apples*
>   3 *tablespoons unsalted butter*
>   3 *tablespoons Calvados or apple brandy*
>   12 *to 14 cornichons or other tart pickle, chopped*

1. Preheat oven to 350° F.

2. Place fish in buttered baking dish and cover with parchment paper. Bake until fish is cooked (10 to 15 minutes). Let cool. Break into 6 or 12 pieces.

3. Put crackers in a bowl and cover with cold water for 5 minutes. Drain and press gently to remove some of the water.

4. In a frying pan render salt pork and fry until brown. Add fish to pan and fry 2 minutes on each side. Add crackers and potatoes. Cover and cook over medium heat, shaking the pan gently from time to time. Turn fish with a spatula. After 20 to 25 minutes of cooking, the fish will break up, the crackers will turn crusty brown, and the potatoes will be done. Season with salt and pepper, then sprinkle with parsley.

5. Peel and core apples. Slice into ½-inch pieces. Heat butter in frying pan. Add apples and sauté until they begin to soften. Warm Calvados or brandy, then pour on apples and ignite; the mixture will flame until the alcohol burns off.

6. Serve fish and potatoes with a small serving of apples and a sprinkling of cornichon.

Serves 6 to 8.

RED SNAPPER AND SHRIMP GUMBO

This gumbo calls for a lot of stirring, but be assured that the taste—especially on the day after preparation—will reward you. It is traditionally served with a spoonful of rice in each bowl.

>   4 *tablespoons lard*
>   1 *pound okra*
>   1 *can (8 oz) tomato sauce*
>   3 *tablespoons lard*
>   5 *tablespoons flour*
>   2½ *cups chopped yellow onion (½-inch pieces)*
>   3 *ribs celery, chopped in ½-inch pieces*
>   1 *green bell pepper, seeded and chopped in ½-inch pieces*
>   1 *clove garlic, minced*
>   7 *cups water*
>   2 *pounds shrimp*
>   1 *pound red snapper or red fish*
>   *Salt*
>   3 *to 4 teaspoons cayenne pepper*
>   *Hot-pepper sauce to taste*

1. Heat the 4 tablespoons lard in a medium saucepan. Add okra and cook for about 10 minutes, stirring occasionally. Add tomato sauce and stir together. Continue to cook until mixture thickens slightly.

2. In a large pot heat the 3 tablespoons lard. Sprinkle flour onto lard and stir. Cook slowly over low heat until mixture turns the color of peanut butter. This mixture of lard and flour is a roux, and will be used to thicken the gumbo. While roux is still hot, add onion, celery, pepper, and garlic. Stir for a few minutes, cover, and turn off heat. Let sit for about 10 minutes.

3. Uncover pan and add 4 cups of the water. Over low heat thicken contents by simmering for 3 to 5 minutes. Add remaining 3 cups water and simmer about 30 minutes. Stir in okra mixture. Add shrimp and fish. Season with salt, cayenne, and hot-pepper sauce. Cook until fish and shrimp are done (10 to 15 minutes).

Serves 8 to 10.

SQUID MARINARA

This flavorful squid dish may be eaten hot or cold. It also makes a wonderful sauce for pasta.

>   4 *pounds squid*
>   ⅓ *cup fruity olive oil*
>   4 *cloves garlic, minced*
>   4 *cups crushed tomatoes in purée*
>   1 *teaspoon dried oregano (not powdered)*
>   1 *teaspoon dried basil or 6 fresh basil leaves*
>   *Salt and freshly ground black pepper*
>   ¼ *cup chopped Italian parsley*
>   1 *teaspoon red pepper flakes*

1. Clean squid (see page 11). Cut the bodies crosswise into ¾-inch pieces. Also cut the tentacles if they are large.

2. In a heavy casserole or Dutch oven, heat oil. Add squid and sauté for 5 to 6 minutes. Add garlic and stir for 1 minute.

3. Add tomato, oregano, basil, salt, and pepper. Cover and allow to cook until squid are tender (about 20 minutes). Stir in parsley and red pepper flakes. Adjust seasonings to taste.

Serves 8.

BRAISED CRABMEAT LION'S HEAD

This northern Chinese dish is traditionally made with pork only. The three patties represent a lion's head. This is an excellent winter dish. Serve with steamed rice.

- 1 pound ground pork
- 2 tablespoons dry sherry
- 2 green onions, minced
- 3 tablespoons minced peeled ginger
- 2 eggs
- 1 teaspoon salt
- ¼ teaspoon pepper
- 1 pound crabmeat
- 4 tablespoons peanut oil
- 2 pounds Napa cabbage or bok choy, shredded
- 2 green onions, slivered (4-inch strips; include part of green)
- 1 cup chicken stock
- 2 tablespoons soy sauce
- ½ teaspoon salt
- ¼ teaspoon pepper

1. Preheat oven to 350° F.

2. Combine pork, sherry, the minced green onion, 2 tablespoons of the ginger, eggs, the 1 teaspoon salt, and first ¼ teaspoon pepper and mix well. Add crab and mix together. Form into 3 large patties.

3. In a large skillet heat peanut oil. Brown patties on both sides.

4. Place cabbage in large casserole dish. Sprinkle the remaining 1 tablespoon ginger and the slivered green onion over cabbage. Place patties on top of cabbage.

5. Heat stock with soy sauce, the ½ teaspoon salt, and second ¼ teaspoon pepper. Pour over cabbage and cover tightly. Braise in oven for 45 to 50 minutes.

Serves 6 to 8.

Served with pasta and bread to absorb all the wonderful sauce, Squid Marinara is flavorful, colorful, and extremely economical. If you've been doubtful about trying squid, this recipe might change your mind.

*Mussel Soup With Red Wine
proves that red wine and seafood
can complement each other.
The red wine gives the
soup a rich, deep flavor.*

MUSSEL SOUP WITH RED WINE

Serve this rich soup with the mussels in or out of the shells. Accompany with a *gougère* (a pastry made with choux paste and Gruyère cheese).

6 to 8 pounds mussels
6 cups Fish Fumet (page 17)
4 tablespoons butter
1 medium onion, chopped
1 medium carrot, chopped in ¼-inch dice
1 rib celery, chopped
1 clove garlic, minced
6 fresh basil leaves or 1 tablespoon dried
6 black peppercorns, bruised
4 cups red wine (Pinot Noir is a good choice)
Salt and pepper
4 tablespoons unsalted butter, softened, kneaded with 4 tablespoons flour (beurre manié)
Basil (for garnish)

1. Scrub and debeard mussels (see page 10). Place in large kettle with 2 cups of the Fish Fumet. Cover and cook over moderate heat, shaking the pan from time to time. The mussels should open after 6 to 8 minutes. Discard any shells that do not open. Remove mussels and discard all but 16 shells; reserve these for garnish. Strain the fumet you used to cook mussels and add more to total 6 cups.

2. In another large kettle melt butter. Add onion, carrot, celery, garlic, basil, and peppercorns. Stir and cook over low heat until vegetables begin to soften. Add fumet and wine and bring to a boil. Allow to boil, uncovered, until reduced to 8 cups.

3. Strain mixture into a clean pot. Season with salt and pepper. Over medium-low heat, whisk in the beurre manié to provide body.

4. Return mussels to pan and reheat. Serve in warm soup plates, garnished with shells, a generous amount of basil, and pepper.

Serves 6 to 8.

CORN AND CRAB SOUP

This soup is a variation of a traditional Cantonese recipe. Canton was a port of entry to China and the setting for much cultural exchange. Corn is not native to China, but the Chinese soon put it to good use.

2 tablespoons unsalted butter
2 tablespoons minced shallot
2 cups fresh corn (may substitute frozen)
3 cups chicken stock
1½ cups half-and-half
Salt and freshly ground white pepper
1 teaspoon sugar (use only if corn is not sweet)
2 large eggs
2 tablespoons water
½ teaspoon salt
1 cup crab claw meat
2 green onions, minced (for garnish)

1. In an 8- to 10-quart kettle, heat butter. Add shallots and sauté until soft. Add corn and stir to coat with butter. Add chicken stock and bring to a simmer. Allow to cook, covered, for 3 to 4 minutes.

2. Stir in half-and-half. Heat through and add salt and pepper to taste. Add sugar if corn isn't as sweet as you expect.

3. Beat eggs with the water and the ½ teaspoon salt. Pour eggs in a stream into hot soup, stirring constantly. Turn off heat and allow eggs to poach into threads.

4. Add crab and allow to heat through from the heat of the soup. Serve with onion as a garnish.

Serves 6 to 8.

NEW ENGLAND CLAM CHOWDER

As is the case with any traditional clam chowder, the amount of salt you add depends on the saltiness of the clam broth and salt pork; be sure to taste before seasoning.

1 quart shucked clams or 20 medium-sized clams, scrubbed and steamed
2 tablespoons butter
¼ pound salt pork, rinsed in cold water and diced finely
1½ cups diced onion
8 cups clam broth
3 cups peeled, cubed potatoes, cooked in salted water
3 cups half-and-half
Salt and freshly ground white pepper
Butter
Oyster crackers or pilot crackers

1. Scrub and steam clams. If necessary, remove and discard shells. Strain clam broth and reserve.

2. In a large kettle place the 2 tablespoons butter with salt pork. Cook over low heat to render fat and brown pork. Remove pork pieces (cracklings) with slotted spoon and reserve.

3. Add onions to fat and cook until they begin to soften. Add clam broth to the kettle and bring to a boil. Reduce heat and simmer for 5 minutes. Chop clams into small pieces and add to kettle along with cooked potatoes.

4. Cover and simmer for 10 minutes. Add half-and-half to kettle and heat gently. Return pork cracklings to pan and season to taste with salt and pepper.

5. Serve in warm bowls with a pat of butter in each bowl and plenty of freshly ground pepper. Pass the crackers.

Serves 8.

MISSOURI CATFISH STEW WITH CORNMEAL WEDGES

Catfish farming is a growing business, so it is fairly easy to find fresh catfish across the country. Cornmeal wedges complement this stew and help make an attractive presentation.

    ¼ pound bacon
    3 large onions, chopped
    2 ribs celery, sliced in ¼-inch
      pieces
    2 carrots, peeled and sliced
      in ¼-inch pieces
    3 cups water
    2 cans (1 lb each) tomato purée
      or 2 pounds fresh tomatoes,
      peeled, seeded, and chopped
    3 cups diced potatoes
      (¼-inch cubes)
    1 tablespoon Worcestershire
      sauce
    ½ teaspoon hot-pepper sauce
    2 teaspoons salt
      Freshly ground pepper to taste
    2 pounds catfish fillets, skinned
      and boned
    2 tablespoons lemon juice

Cornmeal Wedges

    3 cups milk
    1 cup yellow cornmeal
    1 teaspoon salt
    ½ teaspoon pepper

1. Prepare Cornmeal Wedges. In a 5-quart Dutch oven, fry bacon until crisp. Drain on paper towels and crumble. Reserve.

2. Add onions, celery, and carrots to the bacon fat in the pan. Cook until soft (about 5 minutes).

3. Add water, tomato purée, potatoes, Worcestershire sauce, and hot-pepper sauce. Season lightly with salt and pepper.

4. Simmer for 20 to 30 minutes. Add bacon, catfish, and lemon juice and simmer gently for 10 minutes.

5. Ladle stew over Cornmeal Wedges and serve.

Serves 6 to 8.

Cornmeal Wedges In a medium saucepan bring milk to a boil, reduce heat, and add cornmeal in a steady stream, whisking in order to prevent lumps from forming. Continue to whisk until mixture is smooth and thick. Remove pan from heat. Add salt and pepper. Pour mixture into a buttered 9-inch round pan and cool. (It will solidify as it cools.) When cool, brown top of mixture under the broiler. Cut into wedges and serve with catfish stew.

ABALONE STEW

The classic use for abalone is as a steak quickly sautéed in butter for less than a minute on each side. This stew gives another savory use for these univalves. Fresh abalone needs to be pounded to tenderize it, but if frozen or canned, that has been done.

    1 pound abalone steaks
    ⅓ cup unsalted butter
    1 cup finely chopped onion
    1 large clove garlic, peeled
      and minced
    ⅓ cup finely chopped red or
      green bell pepper
    1 bay leaf
    1 can (8 oz) tomato sauce
    2 cups water
    3 potatoes, peeled and cut in
      ½-inch cubes
    ½ teaspoon salt
    ⅓ teaspoon cayenne pepper

1. Cut abalone in ½-inch cubes; reserve. In a large saucepan over medium heat, melt butter and sauté onion, garlic, and pepper until onion is soft and pale gold in color (about 5 minutes). Add bay leaf, tomato sauce, water, potatoes, salt, and cayenne.

2. Cover and simmer until potatoes are almost tender (about 15 minutes). Add abalone cubes and simmer until abalone is tender (4 to 5 minutes).

Serves 8.

SEAFOOD STEW

A bright light in my San Francisco neighborhood is Donna Katzl's Café For All Seasons. This recipe is typical of her cooking, a sensitive handling of fresh ingredients. Serve with plain rice or capelleni pasta.

    ½ cup olive oil
    1¼ cups slivered yellow onion
    ¾ cup thinly sliced carrots
    ¾ cup sliced green onion
      (½-inch slices)
    1 cup peeled, seeded, chopped
      fresh tomatoes
    1½ tablespoons peeled, chopped
      fresh garlic
    1½ cups thinly sliced fresh
      mushrooms
    1⅓ cups dry white wine
    12 ounces red snapper, cut
      in 1-inch chunks
    16 medium-sized shrimp
    12 ounces bay scallops
    24 mussels, cleaned, debearded,
      and scrubbed
    ¼ cup unsalted butter
      Salt and freshly ground
      pepper
    4 or 5 dashes hot-pepper sauce
    ¼ cup chopped parsley
    2 lemons, each cut in 6 wedges

1. Heat olive oil in large skillet (choose one with a lid). Add onion, carrots, green onion, tomatoes, garlic, and mushrooms. Toss and mix until heated.

2. Add wine and heat again until very hot. Add snapper, shrimp, scallops, and mussels. Cover skillet and shake gently, from side to side and up and down, firmly holding cover. In 3 to 4 minutes, mussels will open.

3. Uncover, add butter in pieces, salt, pepper, and hot-pepper sauce. Cover and toss gently for about 30 seconds.

4. Place in 4 bowls. Top each with parsley and place lemon wedges around dishes.

Serves 4.

A flavorful medley of fish, shellfish, and vegetables, Seafood Stew is a light rendition of an old classic. Even non-fish-lovers will approve.

Fresh whole fish can make a spectacular presentation for your dinner. If you've never cooked a whole fish before, try Classic Baked Fish on page 38.

Baking, Broiling, Grilling & Smoking

There are many ways to cook with dry heat: baking, broiling, grilling, and smoking. Whatever the means, the goal is the same: cooking without robbing the food of moisture. Some fish, such as bluefish and mackerel, have a high internal fat or oil content and are especially well suited for dry-heat cooking because they baste themselves. Most fish and shellfish, however, have little internal fat to keep them moist during cooking, and you must take precautions to ensure that they do not dry out.

KEEPING COOKED SEAFOOD MOIST

There are many ways to keep fish and shellfish moist during cooking: (1) wrapping with grape leaves, leafy greens, foil, or parchment paper; (2) covering with vegetables, gratin, or another coating; (3) marinating and basting; (4) stuffing, and (5) leaving on the head and tail. All of these methods accomplish the same purpose: protecting the delicate proteins of the fish from the intense, dry heat of these cooking techniques. Note, however, that the different protective coatings also have different flavorings, so you will want to select the one that works with whatever recipe you are using.

The Canadian Department of Fisheries guide, explained on page 13, remains an acceptable method for timing dry-heat cooking methods such as baking, broiling, and grilling. Smoking has its own set of rules, explained on page 50. The opacity test, also explained on page 13, is the most reliable way to judge if the fish is properly cooked. When the flesh is opaque and does not cling to the bones, the fish is done.

BAKING

Baking is simply roasting fish with dry heat inside an oven. (Don't be confused by a seafood dish called "pan roast," which is a stew prepared on the stove.) Baking gives a cook great latitude in choosing marinades, vegetables, condiments, and herbs to bake along with the fish.

As noted above, protecting the fish from drying out is the prime consideration. Dry heat will bake protected fish to perfection. That same heat will ruin unprotected fish. When preparing baked fish, always preheat the oven. A preheated oven contributes to even cooking.

MULLET IN GRAPE LEAVES

Serve this dish hot or cold. Mullet has a mild, nutty flavor; a rice pilaf with shavings of goat cheese is a wonderful side dish.

> 1 jar (6 to 8 oz) grape leaves, washed
> 6 mullet or other small whole fish
> ½ cup chopped green onion
> ¼ cup chopped parsley
> ¼ cup chopped fresh dill
> 6 tablespoons unsalted butter Salt and freshly ground pepper to taste
> Dry white wine

1. Preheat oven to 425° F. Arrange grape leaves to form 6 rectangular beds. Place 1 fish on each rectangle. Combine green onion, parsley, and dill. Dot fish with butter, and sprinkle with onion-herb mixture, salt, and pepper. Wrap grape leaves around each fish.

2. Place wrapped fish in well-buttered baking dish. Pour in white wine to a depth of ¼ inch. Bake 10 to 20 minutes; baking time depends on thickness of fish.

3. Serve hot or cold. If served cold, add more dill.

Serves 6.

CLASSIC BAKED FISH

This recipe lends itself to the use of any number of sauces (see pages 114 to 122). These sauces can change the flavor of the fish in a variety of interesting ways.

> 1 whole fish (3 to 4 lbs), dressed
> 1½ teaspoons salt
> ½ teaspoon pepper
> Half a lemon, sliced
> ½ cup water

1. Preheat oven to 425° F. Rub fish with salt, pepper, and lemon slices. Use unsalted butter to grease generously a large baking dish. Place fish in the dish and pour in water.

2. Grease parchment paper or foil with unsalted butter and place over fish in baking dish.

3. Bake for 20 to 35 minutes; baking time depends on thickness of fish. Serve with the sauce of your choice.

Serves 4 to 6.

BASS WITH OLIVES

The sauce has a wonderful flavor, so serve plenty of French bread to soak it up. A crisp salad and a glass of Beaujolais complete the feast.

> 1 whole bass (3 to 4 lbs), dressed
> Half a lemon, sliced ¼ inch thick
> ¾ teaspoon salt
> ¼ teaspoon freshly ground pepper
> 4 tablespoons unsalted butter
> 1 medium onion, chopped
> 2 cloves garlic, minced
> 3 tablespoons minced parsley
> 4 large tomatoes, peeled, seeded, and chopped
> ½ cup Fish Fumet (page 17) Fresh oregano
> ¾ cup pitted, sliced green olives
> ½ cup strips of peeled, roasted red peppers or pimiento

1. Preheat oven to 425° F. Score both sides of fish, and place lemon slices in fish cavity. Sprinkle fish with salt and pepper.

2. Melt butter in large sauté pan. Add onion, garlic, parsley, and tomatoes. Cook 5 minutes. Add Fish Fumet and oregano, then cook 10 minutes more. Add olives and peppers.

3. Heavily butter a baking dish large enough to hold bass. Place 1 cup of the tomato mixture in the dish. Place fish on top of mixture, then pour remaining sauce over fish.

4. Bake 20 to 30 minutes; baking time depends on size of fish.

Serves 4 to 6.

Mullet in Grape Leaves is an easy, visually interesting recipe. Although baking is a very easy method of cooking fish, its results can be quite sophisticated.

Cut into the crisp crust of Scallops in Filo to reveal an aromatic and savory filling of scallops, mushrooms, and snow peas in a rich Oriental sauce.

STUFFED TROUT WITH ALMOND BUTTER SAUCE

This is a festive dish that is especially good with new, lightly steamed asparagus. A 6-ounce to 8-ounce trout is often available boned.

    3   tablespoons unsalted butter
    1   small onion, minced
    ½   pound shrimp, shelled,
        deveined, cooked, and
        chopped
    2   tablespoons dry white wine
    2   tablespoons fresh tarragon
        or thyme
    1   tablespoon minced chives
    1½ cups fresh soft bread crumbs
    2   tablespoons cream
    1   egg
        Salt and freshly ground
        pepper to taste
        Freshly ground nutmeg
        to taste
    6   trout (6 to 8 oz each)
    ¼   cup unsalted butter, melted

Almond Butter Sauce

    ½   cup unsalted butter
    ½   cup sliced almonds
    2   teaspoons minced chives
    2   teaspoons lemon juice
        Salt and pepper to taste
        Freshly ground nutmeg
        to taste

1. Preheat oven to 425° F. To make the stuffing, melt the 3 tablespoons butter in large sauté pan. Add onion and cook until soft. Add shrimp and wine. Cook 1 minute. Add tarragon, chives, and bread crumbs; stir to combine. Add cream and egg, and season with salt, pepper, and nutmeg.

2. Stuff trout with bread mixture. Fasten opening with toothpick. Place in large, well-buttered baking dish. Pour the ¼ cup melted butter over fish and cover with buttered foil or parchment paper.

3. Bake 15 to 20 minutes; baking time depends on thickness of fish and stuffing. Serve with Almond Butter Sauce over the trout or to the side.

Serves 6.

Almond Butter Sauce In small pan melt butter, add almonds, and sauté until golden. Remove from heat, then add chives, lemon juice, salt, pepper, and nutmeg. Stir thoroughly, and serve.

MACKEREL PIZZAIOLA

This Italian dish is hearty fare—a good main course. Serve pasta dressed with butter and black pepper as an appetizer.

    1½ tablespoons olive oil
    1   large onion, thinly sliced
    2   cloves garlic, minced
    1½ cups peeled, seeded, and
        chopped tomato
    ½   cup water
    ½   cup minced parsley (prefera-
        bly Italian flat-leaf parsley)
    ½   teaspoon salt
    ¼   teaspoon freshly ground
        black pepper
    3   mackerel, split, heads
        removed, rinsed, and dried
    1   cup fresh soft bread crumbs
    ½   cup freshly grated Parmesan
        cheese

1. Preheat oven to 425° F. In medium sauté pan heat the 1½ tablespoons olive oil. Add onion and garlic. Cook for 1 minute. Add tomato, water, parsley, salt, and pepper; cook for 3 minutes.

2. Grease a large baking dish with additional olive oil. Place fish skin side down in baking dish. Pour tomato mixture over fish. Bake for 15 to 25 minutes; baking time depends on thickness of fish.

3. When fish is cooked, sprinkle bread crumbs and cheese over top, then broil until brown (1 to 2 minutes).

Serves 6.

SCALLOPS IN FILO

This is a wonderful first course by itself or served with spinach sauté. Filo dough tastes best when it is fresh, but frozen dough is perfectly acceptable. Whether fresh or thawed, work quickly so the fragile dough doesn't dry out.

    1   tablespoon dry sherry
    2   tablespoons Fish Fumet
        (page 17)
    2   tablespoons soy sauce
    3   tablespoons julienned peeled
        ginger
    1   tablespoon orange zest
    ¼   teaspoon sesame oil
    ½   pound scallops, cleaned
        and patted dry (if large,
        cut in half)
    6   sheets filo dough
    3   tablespoons unsalted butter,
        melted
    1   leek, white part only,
        julienned
    2   shiitake mushrooms, julienned
        (discard stems)
    4   snow peas, julienned
        Salt and pepper to taste
    1   tablespoon unsalted butter

1. Preheat oven to 425° F. Combine sherry, Fish Fumet, soy sauce, ginger, orange zest (or rind), and sesame oil to form a marinade. Marinate scallops in the mixture for 30 minutes, tossing to coat well.

2. Brush 3 sheets of filo with some of the melted butter. Stack the sheets, turning and offsetting them slightly to form a circle. Make another circle with the remaining 3 sheets of filo. Drain scallops. Place half the scallops on one side of each filo circle.

3. Cover scallops with leeks, shiitake mushrooms, and snow peas. Sprinkle with salt and pepper, and dot with the 1 tablespoon butter. Fold filo over scallops. Tuck edges under and crimp. Brush with remaining melted butter.

4. Place in a large well-buttered baking dish and bake for 12 minutes.

Serves 2.

CATFISH WITH HORSERADISH CREAM

Catfish is a wonderfully sweet-fleshed fish, and the horseradish gives it a zesty flavor. Serve with tiny new potatoes and carrots.

- 2 pounds catfish, skinned, heads removed
- 3 tablespoons lemon juice
  Salt and freshly ground pepper to taste
- 1 tablespoon Dijon mustard
- 2 tablespoons prepared horseradish
- 4 tablespoons sour cream
- ½ cup green onion, chopped (include some of the green portion)

Horseradish Cream

- ½ cup whipping cream, whipped
- 2 tablespoons prepared horseradish
- 1 teaspoon vinegar
  Salt to taste

1. Preheat oven to 425° F. Place fish in a large well-buttered baking dish. Pour lemon juice over fish. Sprinkle with salt and pepper.

2. Combine mustard, horseradish, sour cream, and onion. Spread over fish.

3. Bake 15 to 20 minutes; baking time depends on size of fish.

4. Serve with Horseradish Cream.

Serves 6.

Horseradish Cream In a small bowl combine whipped cream, horseradish, vinegar, and salt. Mix well. Place a dollop of this mixture next to each serving of fish.

FLAMED CRAB WITH NUTTED RICE

This dish has three components that provide intriguing contrasts: a bed of rice with pine nuts, flambéed crab, and a cream sauce. A simple, light salad completes the meal.

- ¼ cup unsalted butter
- 1½ cups long-grain rice
- 2 tablespoons white raisins
- 2 tablespoons pine nuts
- 3 cups chicken stock
- ½ cup unsalted butter
- ¾ cup sliced mushrooms
- 1 tablespoon curry powder
- ¾ teaspoon salt
- ¼ cup freshly ground pepper
- 1½ cups crabmeat
- ¼ cup brandy or Cognac
- ¼ pound Swiss cheese, grated

Cream Sauce

- 6 tablespoons unsalted butter
- ¼ cup flour
- 3 cups milk
- ¼ cup whipping cream
  Salt and freshly ground pepper to taste

1. In a medium saucepan melt the ¼ cup butter, add rice, and stir until rice is completely coated with butter. Stir in raisins and pine nuts, then chicken stock. Cover pan and cook over very low heat until tender, usually about 20 minutes. Add more stock if liquid is absorbed before rice is tender.

2. While rice is cooking, melt the ½ cup butter in a medium frying pan. Sauté mushrooms in butter for 3 to 4 minutes. Add curry powder, salt, pepper, and crab. Mix well.

3. Preheat oven to 425° F. Heat brandy in a small saucepan, pour over crab mixture, and ignite. Brandy will flame until alcohol burns off.

4. In a large, well-buttered baking dish spread half of the rice. Place crab on top, then cover with remaining rice. Pour Cream Sauce over top and sprinkle with cheese. Bake 15 to 18 minutes.

Serves 6 to 8.

Cream Sauce In a medium saucepan melt butter. Whisk in flour, and cook for 2 minutes. Gradually whisk in milk, simmering until sauce thickens. Continue cooking and whisking for 3 minutes. Add cream and season with salt and pepper.

BAKED MACKEREL WITH FENNEL AND PROSCIUTTO

Fennel has a slight flavor of licorice or anise—a crisp taste to complement prosciutto. Sliced tomatoes with chopped fresh basil provide a pleasing accompaniment.

- 3 tablespoons olive oil
- 2 cloves garlic, minced
  Fennel leaves snipped from 2 bulbs of fennel
- 1 cup fresh, soft bread crumbs
- 3 slices prosciutto, slivered
- ½ teaspoon salt
- ¼ teaspoon freshly ground pepper
- 2 mackerel (1½ lbs each)

1. Preheat oven to 425° F. Heat olive oil in a medium frying pan. Add garlic and fennel, and cook 1 minute. Add bread crumbs and prosciutto. Toss to coat with oil. Add salt and pepper and mix well.

2. Cut two deep scores in both sides of each mackerel. Stuff scores with as much bread mixture as possible. Place fish in a large, well-buttered baking dish. Sprinkle remaining bread mixture over fish.

3. Bake for 15 to 20 minutes; baking time depends on thickness of fish. When cooking is complete, place fish under the broiler just long enough to brown topping.

Serves 4 to 6.

BROILED FINNAN HADDIE

Since finnan haddie is only lightly smoked, it requires additional cooking. Serve this dish for breakfast with scrambled eggs or as a late supper with a green salad.

> 1 pound finnan haddie
> Milk, if needed
> ½ pound new potatoes
> 2 tablespoons unsalted butter
> 2 tablespoons lemon juice
> 2 tablespoons minced chives
> 1 tablespoon minced fresh dill
> Freshly ground pepper to taste

1. If haddie is hard or briny and not soft to the touch, soak fish in milk for 2 to 3 hours. Preheat broiler. Slice haddie ¼ inch thick and arrange in large, well-buttered baking dish.

2. Slice potatoes ¼ inch thick and arrange with haddie in baking dish. Dot fish and potatoes with butter. Sprinkle with lemon juice, chives, dill, and freshly ground pepper.

3. Place fish and potatoes under broiler and broil until golden brown.

Serves 4 to 6.

SABLEFISH WITH SAVORY BUTTER

Savory Butter is an excellent addition to any type of broiled fish. Serve with steamed cabbage and pumpernickel.

> *Sablefish fillets (about 1 lb)*

Savory Butter

> ½ cup unsalted butter
> 2 teaspoons anchovy paste
> 2 tablespoons lemon juice
> 2 tablespoons capers

Preheat broiler. Place fillets on broiling pan. Spread some of the Savory Butter over fish. Broil 3 to 5 minutes, depending on thickness of fish. Serve with remaining Savory Butter.

Serves 6.

Savory Butter Place butter, anchovy paste, lemon juice, and capers in bowl of food processor or blender. Process until smooth.

BROILED SALMON WITH SOUFFLÉ TOPPING

If you substitute dried herbs for fresh, use whole leaves instead of pulverized ones. Powdered herbs deteriorate rapidly and have a weaker flavor. Serve this salmon dish with fried green tomatoes.

> ¾ cup unsalted butter
> 1 large shallot, minced
> 2 tablespoons minced fresh tarragon or 1 tablespoon dried
> 1 tablespoon minced fresh dill or ½ tablespoon dried
> 2 tablespoons minced chives
> 6 salmon fillets or steaks

Soufflé Topping

> 1½ cups Basic Mayonnaise (see page 117)
> 2 tablespoons minced fresh tarragon or 1 tablespoon dried
> 1 tablespoon minced fresh dill or ½ tablespoon dried
> 2 tablespoons minced chives
> 2 egg whites

1. Preheat broiler. In a small saucepan melt butter. Add shallot, tarragon, dill, and chives. Place salmon in a large, heat-resistant gratin dish, and brush it with the herb butter. Broil 10 minutes or until fish is cooked; broiling time depends on thickness of fish.

2. Cover the salmon with Soufflé Topping. Broil until puffy and brown, 2 to 3 minutes.

Serves 6.

Soufflé Topping In a small bowl combine mayonnaise, tarragon, dill, and chives. Mix well. Beat egg whites until stiff but not dry. Fold egg whites into mayonnaise mixture. Cover salmon with topping before broiling.

JAPANESE-STYLE COD

Steamed rice and Cucumber Salad complete this classic Japanese presentation.

> ¼ cup julienned peeled ginger
> 2 cloves garlic, minced
> 2 tablespoons soy sauce
> 4 tablespoons dry sherry
> ½ teaspoon sugar
> ½ cup Fish Fumet (page 17) or clam juice
> 6 dashes hot-pepper sauce
> 2 tablespoons dark sesame oil
> 2 tablespoons minced green onion
> 6 pieces of cod, totaling about 2 pounds

Cucumber Salad

> 3 tablespoons Japanese rice wine vinegar
> 3 tablespoons corn oil
> 1 tablespoon soy sau[ce]
> 1 teaspoon sugar
> 1 English (hothouse) cucumber sliced paper-thin; do not peel

1. In a medium saucepan combine ginger, garlic, soy sauce, sherry, sugar, Fish Fumet, hot-pepper sauce, oil, and onion. Bring to a boil, reduce heat and simmer for 1 m[inute].

2. Brush cod fillets with sauce and marinate for 30 minutes.

3. Preheat broiler. Place fish on broiling pan and broil 8 to 12 minutes; broiling time depends on thickness of fish. Turn fish halfway through cooking time. Brush with remaining sauce and serve with Cucumber Salad.

Serves 6.

Cucumber Salad Combine vinegar, oil, soy sauce, and sugar. Pour over cucumbers and toss, coating cucumbers well.

Plump raw oysters are an elegant first-course or buffet treat. Enterprising individuals on the West Coast have recently begun to farm these popular bivalves, increasing their availability.

SWORDFISH PAILLARD WITH SALSA

In this recipe, *paillard* refers to a large, thin slice of fish. Serve with tortilla chips or warm corn tortillas.

- 6 swordfish steaks, cut ½ inch thick
- 3 tablespoons unsalted butter, melted
- 1 teaspoon salt
- ½ teaspoon freshly ground pepper

Salsa

- 3 large tomatoes, chopped and drained
- 1 small onion, chopped fine
- 2 to 4 serrano or jalapeño chiles, chopped fine, including seeds
- 1 tablespoon lime juice, or more to taste
- 1 bunch cilantro
  Salt to taste

1. Preheat broiler. Brush fish with butter and sprinkle with salt and pepper.

2. Broil fish 4 inches from heat for 1½ minutes. Turning the fish is unnecessary. Serve with Salsa.

Serves 6.

Salsa Combine tomatoes, onion, peppers, lime juice, cilantro, and salt. Correct seasonings, adding more lime juice and salt, if needed.

STURGEON BROCHETTE WITH HONEY MUSTARD SAUCE

A brochette is usually served on a bed of rice. Try delicious Onion and Rice Soubise instead.

  4 sturgeon steaks (6 oz each),
       cut in 6 to 8 equal pieces
  1 cup whipping cream
  3 tablespoons dry white wine
  1 tablespoon honey
  1 tablespoon coarse-grain
       mustard

Onion and Rice Soubise

  2 pounds white onions
  3 tablespoons unsalted butter
  ¾ cup rice
  2 cups Fish Fumet (page 17)
       or chicken stock
  1 teaspoon salt
  ⅓ teaspoon white pepper
  ⅓ cup whipping cream
  2 tablespoons unsalted butter

1. Preheat broiler. Place fish on skewers.

2. In a small saucepan over medium-high heat, reduce cream by half. Watch carefully to prevent cream from boiling over. When reduced add wine, honey, and mustard. Mix well, simmer 1 minute, remove from heat.

3. Brush sturgeon with sauce. Place fish on baking sheet and broil 2 to 3 minutes, turning once. Serve with remaining sauce on a bed of Onion and Rice Soubise.

Serves 4 to 6.

Onion and Rice Soubise Peel and coarsely slice onions. Melt the 3 tablespoons butter in pan, add onions, and cook for 5 to 7 minutes. Add rice, mix well, then add fumet, salt, and pepper. Cover and simmer 30 minutes. Purée the mixture in a food processor, adding cream and the 2 tablespoons butter. Reheat over low heat. Adjust seasonings and serve.

GRILLING

Grilling is one of the earliest techniques of fish cookery. The cook placed the fish on a spit or held it over an open fire. The Eskimos and the Indians of the American Northwest provided an interesting variation. They cooked fish on a stick of sweet bark pushed into the ground next to the hot coals. *Planking* is another variation of grilling. A split fish is nailed to a nonresinous hardwood board. The board is angled toward the fire and serves as a platter after the fish is cooked.

Exact grilling times are difficult to predict because of the extreme variability of the elements involved—the heat of the coals, the distance between the coals and the grill, and the type of coals. A rule of thumb is to place the grill 4 to 6 inches above the heat source. If you use mesquite charcoal, remember that it burns two to three times hotter than charcoal briquettes, a factor that has a critical effect on the short cooking time essential for succulent grilled fish.

One clever technique is to bring the charcoal to the point where grilling would normally begin, then arrange the coals to outline the fish, leaving ashes directly under the fish. Using this method, oil or marinade will not fall onto live coals and burst into flames. Hinged basket grills, which clamp over fish, lessen the problem of turning the fish on a grill. Fish steaks and fillets fit into a rectangular grilling basket; whole fish require a fish-shaped grilling basket. If you do not use a basket, two broad spatulas will help turn fish without breaking them.

Before grilling, oil both the grill and the fish. Heat the grill or grilling basket before placing the fish on or in them. When grilling a whole fish, make shallow slashes in the skin to prevent it from drawing up. Adding chips of moist wood, such as apple, maple, hickory, or cherry, will impart a slightly smoked taste to the fish.

GRILLED OYSTERS, ONIONS, AND RADICCHIO WITH MIGNONETTE SAUCE

These plump morsels are often served by themselves as a first course, followed by a spicy sausage or full red-meat course. If used as a main course, serve them with grilled onions and radicchio.

 24 oysters in the shell
  2 large onions
  2 heads radicchio
       Olive oil

Mignonette Sauce

  ¾ cup white wine vinegar
  ¾ cup dry white wine
  3 shallots, minced
  1 teaspoon freshly ground
       black pepper
  2 teaspoons minced parsley

1. *To prepare oysters:* Prepare coals. Scrub oysters. Place them with the deeper shell on grill. During cooking oysters open only a crack, not wide like clams. When oysters open, remove them from grill.

2. *To prepare onions and radicchio:* Peel onions and slice in half, leaving root core intact to hold onion together. Brush onions and radicchio with olive oil and grill until radicchio begins to wilt and onions begin to soften.

3. Serve oysters on a platter with Mignonette Sauce in the center and onions and radicchio on the side.

Serves 6 to 8.

Mignonette Sauce In a medium bowl combine vinegar, wine, shallots, pepper, and parsley. Mix well.

BLUEFISH WITH MELON SALSA

This recipe comes from Steve Simmons, a talented young chef and a graduate of City College Culinary Program in San Francisco. His broad knowledge of cookery and understanding of flavor combinations are evident in this example of grilling. Corn husks are available in Mexican markets.

- *1 package corn husks*
- *4 bluefish fillets (7 oz each)*
  Oil
- *2 tablespoons lemon juice*
- *½ cup dry white wine*
- *1 cup soy sauce*
- *¼ cup stone-ground mustard*
- *1 teaspoon freshly ground black pepper*
- *1 teaspoon minced garlic*
- *3 bay leaves*
- *4 lemons, sliced ¼ inch thick*
- *¼ cup julienned red onion*
- *2 cups julienned leeks (optional)*
  Freshly ground pepper to taste
  Sprigs of watercress
  (for garnish)

Melon Salsa

- *1 cup casaba melon cut in ¼-inch dice*
- *1 cup honeydew melon cut in ¼-inch dice*
- *1 cup Crenshaw melon cut in ¼-inch dice*
- *½ cup chopped papaya (optional)*
- *1 tablespoon chopped fresh mint*
- *1 teaspoon minced jalapeño pepper*
- *1 teaspoon cider vinegar*
- *1 teaspoon lemon juice*

1. Cover corn husks with water and let stand for 45 minutes until they are soft and pliable.

2. Trim fillets, removing skin and oily meats on sides. Rinse with water and pat dry. Sprinkle with 1 tablespoon of the lemon juice.

3. Mix wine, soy sauce, mustard, remaining 1 tablespoon lemon juice, the 1 teaspoon pepper, garlic, bay leaves, and lemon slices. Add half of the onions to the mixture. Marinate the fish in this mixture for 30 minutes.

4. Prepare coals. In another bowl combine remaining onions and leeks (if used).

5. Arrange 2 or 3 corn husks lengthwise to form a rectangle. Make 4 rectangles. Place equal amounts of leek-and-onion mixture onto each rectangle. Place a marinated fillet lengthwise on each rectangle. Add pepper to taste.

6. Wrap fillets as you would a package, completely enclosing fish in corn husks. Tie corn husks with ⅛-inch cord—2 cords across the bulk of the fillet and 1 cord lengthwise—with the knot on the bottom of the package. The top should be smooth string.

7. Begin grilling when coals are white-hot, not smoking. Brush the packages with a light coating of oil to prevent sticking. Place the smooth side down first. Grill each side for 5 to 7 minutes. If corn husks begin to burn or dry, brush with more oil.

8. To serve, cut a cross through the smooth side of the packages, and pull back the corners of corn husks slightly. Garnish with a sprig of watercress. Serve with Melon Salsa.

Serves 4.

Melon Salsa In a large bowl combine all ingredients. Cover the bowl because melons are susceptible to foreign odors, and refrigerate the mixture until serving.

GRILLED TUNA

A summertime specialty, this dish is a whole meal in itself. The variety of vegetables creates a colorful medley. To vary the effect substitute broccoli, carrots, cauliflower, celery, sugar snap peas, baby squash, or another vegetable that seems enticing. Vary the quantities of individual ingredients according to your taste.

- *1 bunch asparagus*
- *2 bulbs fennel, quartered*
- *½ pound snow peas*
- *8 quarts boiling salted water*
- *3 red, yellow, or green bell peppers*
- *1 basket cherry tomatoes*
- *4 tuna steaks (6 to 8 oz each)*
  Olive oil

Vinaigrette Sauce

- *½ cup vegetable oil*
- *½ cup fruity olive oil*
- *¼ cup red wine vinegar*
- *1 tablespoon balsamic vinegar*
- *2 teaspoons Dijon mustard*
- *1 clove garlic, minced*
- *1 teaspoon salt*
- *¼ teaspoon freshly ground black pepper*

1. Prepare coals. Trim asparagus, fennel, and snow peas. Blanch these vegetables in the boiling water, then plunge them into ice water to stop cooking. Drain and set aside.

2. Core and cut peppers into strips. Remove stems from tomatoes and leave whole. Set aside.

3. Brush steaks with oil and grill 3 to 7 minutes per side; grilling time depends on size of steaks.

4. Place tuna steaks on platter. Surround with vegetables. Drizzle Vinaigrette Sauce over top.

Serves 6 to 8.

Vinaigrette Sauce Combine oils, vinegars, mustard, garlic, salt, and pepper. Mix well.

GRILLED HALIBUT

Halibut is a firm-fleshed fish that
blends well with a variety of flavors.
Serve with Grilled Eggplant Salad.

1½ pounds halibut, cut into cubes
    Cubes of French bread, crusts
    removed
    Whole fresh sage leaves
    Salt and freshly ground
    pepper
¼ cup olive oil
¼ cup lemon juice

Grilled Eggplant Salad

1 large eggplant (1½ lbs)
2 large tomatoes
1 green bell pepper, seeded
   and finely chopped
½ cup minced onion
2 cloves garlic, minced
1 teaspoon salt
½ teaspoon freshly ground
   pepper
3 tablespoons red wine vinegar
⅓ cup olive oil
   Chopped parsley (for garnish)

1. Prepare coals. Thread halibut,
bread, and sage leaves onto skewers.
Sprinkle with salt and pepper.

2. Mix together olive oil and lemon
juice. Brush halibut and bread with
this mixture.

3. Grill for 10 to 20 minutes, turning
and brushing with oil and lemon
juice until bread is browned.

Serves 4 to 6.

Grilled Eggplant Salad Grill eggplant until skin is blackened and
charred; cool and remove skin by
rubbing with damp paper towels.
Finely chop eggplant. Place tomatoes
on grill and cook until skin is
charred. Cool and coarsely chop. In a
medium bowl combine eggplant, tomatoes, pepper, onion, and garlic.
Mix well. Combine salt, pepper, vinegar, and olive oil. Mix with eggplant
mixture and chill. Garnish with
chopped parsley and serve.

*Grilled Tuna can be
served on its own, as
shown here, or on top of a
bountiful assortment of
fresh garden vegetables to
make a spectacular salad.*

GRILLED GULF COAST RED SNAPPER WITH MARIGOLD MINT BUTTER SAUCE

This recipe comes from Stephan Pyles, chef at Routh Street Cafe in Dallas, Texas. Stephan has an incredible palate and creates innovative, exciting dishes.

To add another element to the collage of flavors, soak six to eight chunks of mesquite, hickory, or other aromatic wood in water. While the chunks soak, build a medium-hot fire with hardwood charcoal briquettes. After 20 to 30 minutes, add the soaked chunks to the fire and let them burn for 10 minutes before grilling the snapper.

4 Gulf Coast red snapper
  fillets (8 oz each)
  Olive oil or clarified butter
  Salt and freshly ground
  pepper to taste

Marigold Mint Butter Sauce

⅓ cup pecans, toasted
2 tablespoons unsalted butter,
  softened
1 tablespoon snipped chives
2 serrano chiles, seeded
  and finely diced
⅓ cup Fish Fumet (page 17)
⅓ cup dry white wine
⅓ cup white wine vinegar
1 tablespoon chopped shallot
2 tablespoons Mexican
  marigold mint
1 cup unsalted butter, cut
  in small chunks
1 tablespoon lime juice
  Salt and freshly ground
  pepper to taste

1. Prepare coals. Lightly coat fillets with olive oil or clarified butter. Season with salt and pepper.

2. Grill fish over medium-hot coals for approximately 3 minutes per side. Serve with Marigold Mint Butter Sauce.

Serves 4.

Marigold Mint Butter Sauce

Place pecans in food processor. Process in several stages, turning the machine off for several seconds between each stage. Add the 2 tablespoons butter, chives, and chiles. Blend until smooth, about 2 minutes. Set mixture aside. In a medium saucepan combine fumet, wine, vinegar, shallot, and 1 tablespoon of the marigold mint. Bring to a boil. Reduce mixture until 2 tablespoons remain. Decrease heat and whisk in the 1 cup butter, a piece at a time. When all butter is incorporated, add remaining tablespoon of marigold mint and lime juice. Whisk in pecan mixture and season with salt and pepper. Place sauce in a double boiler over barely simmering water until ready to serve.

SMOKING

Smoking is an ancient dry-heat cooking method. Although there are several ways to smoke fish, for home smoking it is best to use a hot-smoking process. If you're interested in smoking your own fish, buy or build a smoker, and follow the instructions appropriate to your model; the descriptions below only outline the basic steps. The recipes that follow call for smoked fish, either purchased or home-smoked.

Traditional Hot Smoking

Fish destined for hot smoking must first be soaked in salted water, a process called brining. Kosher salt extracts excess moisture and firms the flesh of the fish. (Do not use table salt—it contains chemical additives that inhibit the process and leave a bitter taste.) A typical brining solution consists of 2 cups of salt and 4 cups of water. If desired, add 1 cup brown sugar, herbs of your choice, garlic, and shallots to flavor the brining liquid.

Brining time depends on the size of the fish and the smoking method: Traditional hot smoking requires 30 minutes to 8 hours of brining. Fillets take less time than a whole fish. Longer brining yields smokier, drier fish with longer shelf life.

After brining, wash the fish thoroughly and hang it in a cool place to dry. Use a fan if you wish. Dry the fish until a pellicle—a thin, shiny skin—forms on the surface. The pellicle seals in natural juices. Drying takes 30 minutes for fillets to several hours for large whole fish.

When the fish has dried, it is ready to hot smoke. Different types of smoking wood, such as apple, cherry, alder, and hickory, lend interesting flavors and aromas to the fish.

Smoking time ranges from a few hours to a few days. It depends on the degree of smokiness desired, the heat of the smoke inside the smoker, and the weather. Most smokers are not insulated, so if the weather is cold outside, the heat inside the smoker is not as intense. Most whole fish can be ready to eat within a few hours. Smoked fish is done when it flakes at the bone. Use a two-pronged, long fork to test it.

A Hot Smoking Shortcut

A shorter form of hot smoking consists of brining the fish for 30 minutes to 2 hours, eliminating the drying phase, and hot smoking it for 1½ to 2 hours at a higher temperature. Fish smoked this way will taste less smoky, and have a shorter shelf life.

Water Smoking

Water smoking is a method that combines smoking and steaming and requires a pan of liquid above the heat source and below the smoking rack. Many smokers now come equipped with a water pan. Juices from the fish fall into the liquid and return to the fish in the form of flavored steam. Wine, herbs, or citrus peels enhance the character of the steam, and wood chips add another flavor dimension. Water smoking is a faster process than hot smoking but is a cooking method, not a preservation method.

When the smoking process is completed, remove the head and dried skin of the fish and lift the wonderfully flavored smoked meat away from the bones.

Delicious Smoked Trout Mousse can be served alone, garnished with red caviar as shown here, or with golden caviar and Beurre Blanc.

SMOKED FISH PÂTÉ

Better cheese shops sell fresh cream cheese. It has a wonderful taste absent from the packaged cream cheese that supermarkets sell. Serve this pâté as an appetizer with crisp crackers.

    Half a small onion
    ¼ cup parsley
    ¼ cup unsalted butter
    8 ounces fresh cream cheese
    10 ounces smoked fish
    3 tablespoons lemon juice
    1 tablespoon Dijon mustard
    6 drops hot-pepper sauce
       White pepper
       Salt

1. In a food processor fitted with a steel blade, mince onion and parsley. Add butter, cheese, fish, lemon juice, mustard, hot-pepper sauce, pepper, and salt. Purée until smooth.

2. Pack purée into a serving crock and chill at least 2 hours.

Serves 8.

CHINESE TEA-SMOKED FISH

The fish in this dish is smoked in a wok and has an unusual, delicious flavor of tea. Tea-smoked fish is served as one of many entrées in a traditional Chinese meal.

    ½ cup dark brown sugar
    ½ cup uncooked rice
    ¼ cup black tea leaves
    8 to 10 green onions
    1 steamed fish, about 2 pounds
       Sesame oil

1. Line a large wok with heavy-duty foil. Place sugar, rice, and tea leaves in the bottom. Oil a rack and place it over sugar, rice, and tea.

2. Arrange onions along the rack and place fish on top. Cover wok, and coil wet towels around the edge. Set wok over medium-high heat for 2 to 3 minutes, then turn heat to low. Smoke fish for about 10 minutes.

Uncover wok outdoors if possible. Turn fish over, cover, and smoke for 5 to 8 more minutes.

3. Remove fish, brush with oil, and serve whole.

Serves 4 to 6.

SMOKED TROUT MOUSSE WITH GOLDEN CAVIAR AND BEURRE BLANC

This is an elegant recipe made easy by the food processor. Donna Nordin, a San Francisco cooking teacher of note, created this dish, which serves as a delightful first course or wonderful luncheon treat. Serve with tiny glazed onions.

    8 sprigs fresh dill
    1 pound smoked trout meat
    3 egg whites
    1⅓ cups cold whipping cream
       Salt
       White pepper
    1 tablespoon minced fresh dill
    2 tablespoons golden caviar
       Sprigs of dill (for garnish)

Beurre Blanc

    1 shallot, minced
    ¼ cup dry white wine
    ¼ cup white wine vinegar
    ½ cup unsalted butter
       Salt and pepper to taste

1. Preheat oven to 350° F. Butter eight ½-cup round molds. Place a sprig of dill in the center bottom of each mold.

2. In a food processor fitted with a steel blade, process trout until very finely ground. Add egg whites and process. With machine running, pour in cream in a slow, steady stream. Season with salt, pepper, and minced dill.

3. Fill buttered molds ¾-inch full. Place molds in baking pan, and pour hot water into pan almost to the top of the molds. Bake until the top springs back to the touch, about 15 to 20 minutes.

4. To serve, place some of the Beurre Blanc on a warm platter, unmold mousse on top, and sprinkle with caviar. Garnish with dill.

Serves 8.

Beurre Blanc In a small saucepan place shallot, wine, and vinegar. Cook over high heat until only 2 tablespoons of liquid remain. Remove from heat and beat in butter bit by bit. Season with salt and pepper.

RILLETTES OF SWORDFISH

Classic French rillettes are pieces of meat or poultry cooked in fat, seasoned, then pounded in a mortar. Pounding creates a textured effect, which is achieved in this dish by shredding the swordfish. Serve rillettes as an appetizer or first course with thin slices of melba toast.

    1 pound smoked swordfish
    10 tablespoons unsalted butter
       at room temperature
    ¼ cup chopped onion
    1 clove garlic, minced
    2 tablespoons dry white wine
    1 teaspoon lime juice
    1 teaspoon salt
    ¼ teaspoon white pepper

1. Shred smoked swordfish. Mix with 8 tablespoons of the unsalted butter.

2. In medium sauté pan, melt the remaining 2 tablespoons butter. Add onion, garlic, wine, and lime juice. Cook until onions are soft and the liquid has evaporated. Cool, then add to swordfish, mixing well. Correct seasonings and add salt and pepper.

3. Cover and refrigerate for at least 4 hours before serving.

Serves 8 to 10 as an appetizer.

*Two favorites of all cuisines—
fresh seafood and garlic—
are the basis for a wide
variety of delicious sautéed and
stir-fried entrées.*

Sautéing, Stir-Frying & Deep-Frying

Sautéing, stir-frying, and deep-frying are different cooking methods that have in common their reliance on the use of fats, a term that includes oils. Sautéing and stir-frying each use a very small amount of fat that often becomes part of the finished dish. Deep-fried food, on the other hand, is totally immersed in fat, which is not served with the final dish. All of these cooking processes use extremely high temperatures; this seals in the flavor and succulence of the fish.

COOKING GUIDELINES

The four most important factors in oil cookery are the choice of cooking fat, the temperature of the fat, the coating of the fish or shellfish, and the cooking time.

Cooking fats range from butter to olive and vegetable oils. Sautés use clarified butter (see page 114). Peanut oil or corn oil are the most common fats for stir-frying. In earlier days cooks usually used an animal fat, such as lard, for deep-frying, but the flavor of the finished dish is too heavy for modern tastes. Today we tend to prefer solid vegetable shortenings, peanut oil, or corn oil. Olive oil is also popular but it has a strong flavor that a cook must take into consideration.

The temperature of the fat is quite critical. If the fat is too cool, the fish will absorb the fat and become soggy and heavy. If the oil is too hot, the outside of the fish will burn before the inside cooks.

Coatings often protect delicate fish and shellfish from the heat. A coating may be a light dusting of flour for sautéing, a coating of cornstarch and egg white for stir-frying, or a heavy batter for deep-frying.

Cooking times can be based on the Canadian Fisheries guidelines and the opacity test, both explained in the "Cooking Rules of Thumb" section on page 13.

SAUTÉING

Sauté means to cook food in a small quantity of very hot fat. The terms *sauté* and *pan-fry* are interchangeable. Sauté is a French term that has no English translation; pan-fry is an English term that has no French translation.

A successful sauté depends on three factors. First, the fat must be hot. If it is not hot enough, the fish will stick to the pan, the outside of the fish will not be seared, and the juices will escape.

Second, the food must be absolutely dry. Moisture on the food forms a layer of steam between the food and the fat that prevents searing and browning.

Third—and many overlook this factor—the pan must not be too crowded. Space between each piece of fish is a prerequisite for thorough browning. Crowding causes fish to steam instead of sear, and the juices from the fish escape into the pan. Just as it is important not to crowd the pan, it is equally important not to use too large a pan. The more the fish covers the fat, the less the chance of the fat burning.

Butter is the most flavorful of fats, but it burns at a relatively low temperature (248° F). The solution is to clarify it (see page 114). Clarification removes the particles of protein and minerals that cause smoking at low temperatures. The end result is a pure fat that can withstand temperatures of up to 375° F.

Restaurant chefs often add a tablespoon or two of cooking oil to unclarified butter to raise the temperature at which it will begin to smoke. Even with the oil, the risk remains that protein particles will blacken and ruin the dish.

A coating protects delicate fish or shellfish from the heat of sautéing and ensures that the outside of the fish is completely dry. Coatings may be of cornmeal, cracker crumbs, bread crumbs, or flour. All these coatings seal in the juices. Preparing a sauté without a coating requires special diligence: The surface of the fish must be dry and the cooking time must be brief. In addition, you must keep the fish in motion in the pan.

ROCKFISH VERACRUZ

This dish can also be made with 1 pound of rockfish and 1 pound of prawns. Serve with hot buttered corn tortillas.

- ½ cup flour
- 2 teaspoons salt
- 1 teaspoon freshly ground pepper
- 2 pounds rockfish fillets
- ¾ cup clarified butter (see page 114)
- 4 to 6 cloves garlic, peeled and slivered
- ¼ cup olive oil
- 2 large onions, sliced in ¼-inch rings
- 2 large bell peppers, sliced in ¼-inch rings
- 4 tomatoes, peeled, seeded, and chopped
- 2 to 3 jalapeño peppers, seeded and cut in thin strips
- 1 avocado, peeled, halved, and sliced in ¼-inch segments

1. Combine flour, 1 teaspoon of the salt, and ½ teaspoon of the pepper. Pat fillets dry, then dust with seasoned flour.

2. In large sauté pan over low heat, melt butter. Add garlic; sauté 1 minute. Add fillets and sauté on each side until golden.

3. Place fish on large, warm serving platter.

4. In another pan heat olive oil. Add onions and cook until they begin to wilt. Add bell peppers, tomatoes, jalapeño peppers, remaining 1 teaspoon salt, and remaining ½ teaspoon pepper. Stir and cook, uncovered, for 5 minutes. Cover and simmer 10 minutes. Correct seasonings.

5. Pour sauce over hot fillets. Place avocado down the center of the fish.

Serves 6 to 8.

Any species of rockfish will work for Rockfish Veracruz. Use red bell peppers in season for a colorful presentation.

Shrimp With Cumin and Orange is a versatile dish that may be served hot or chilled. The cumin powder should be fresh; powdered spices lose their potency over time.

SCALLOPS IN RED WINE SAUCE

Serve this dish with a triangle of puff pastry on each plate along with steamed small new potatoes. The potatoes are delicious when mashed into the sauce.

- ½ cup clarified butter (see page 114)
- ¼ cup minced shallots
- 1 cup peeled, seeded, chopped, drained tomato
- ¼ cup whipping cream
- 2½ pounds large scallops
- ½ cup flour
- 1 teaspoon salt
- ½ teaspoon freshly ground pepper
- 1½ cups light red wine (such as Beaujolais)
- 2 tablespoons unsalted butter
- 3 tablespoons minced chives
- ¼ cup minced parsley

1. In a large sauté pan, melt ¼ cup of the clarified butter. Add shallots and cook until soft. Add tomato, stir, and cook, uncovered, 3 to 4 minutes. Add cream; bring to a boil and reduce for 1 minute. Remove from heat and reserve.

2. Heat remaining ¼ cup clarified butter in large sauté pan. Dust scallops lightly with flour, salt, and pepper. Add scallops and cook for 1 to 2 minutes, shaking pan constantly.

3. With slotted spoon, remove scallops to warm platter. Add wine to the pan and bring to a boil. Reduce mixture by about half. Add tomato mixture and reheat. Add scallops, then reheat gently. Correct seasonings and swirl in the 2 tablespoons butter. Sprinkle with chives and parsley.

Serves 6 to 8.

TROUT SAUTÉ WITH BUTTER AND LEMON

This recipe is a classic *truite sauté meunière* in French cuisine. If you use larger trout, cook them longer and baste with the butter. Serve with shoestring or fried potatoes.

- ½ cup flour
- 1 teaspoon salt
- ½ teaspoon freshly ground pepper
- 6 whole trout (6 to 8 oz each)
- 1 cup milk
- ½ cup clarified butter (see page 114)
- 2 tablespoons unsalted butter
- ½ cup minced parsley
  Juice of 1 large lemon
  Freshly ground pepper

1. Combine flour, salt, and the ½ teaspoon pepper. Dip trout in milk, then in flour mixture. Shake excess flour from fish.

2. In sauté pan heat the ½ cup clarified butter over medium heat. Add trout and sauté until golden brown on each side.

3. Remove fish to a warm platter. Add the 2 tablespoons butter to pan. When it melts and turns a nut-brown color, add parsley and lemon juice. Pour mixture over fish. Sprinkle with freshly ground pepper.

Serves 6.

SHRIMP WITH CUMIN AND ORANGE

Serve this colorful and flavorful dish with pilaf or plain rice. Chill the dish to serve as a first course.

- 2 oranges
- ¼ cup olive oil
- 1½ teaspoons ground cumin
- 1 pound medium shrimp, peeled and deveined
- 1 medium red onion, separated into rings
  Salt
- 1 cup Niçoise olives, drained
  Freshly ground pepper

1. Peel 1 orange and divide into sections. Squeeze and reserve the juice from the other orange.

2. In sauté pan heat olive oil. Add cumin, then immediately add shrimp. Sauté until shrimp just begin to turn pink (2 to 3 minutes).

3. Add onion rings to pan and sauté for 1 to 2 minutes. Sprinkle with salt. Add orange juice and olives. Sauté long enough to heat through.

4. Turn out onto serving plate. Scatter orange segments over top. Sprinkle with pepper.

Serves 4 to 6.

BOURBON SHRIMP

Add pecans to this dish or serve a few toasted salted pecans on the side. Wild rice, with its nutty flavor, is also a fitting accompaniment.

- ¼ cup unsalted butter
- 1 pound shrimp, peeled and deveined
- ¼ cup bourbon
- ¼ cup whipping cream
- 1 teaspoon tomato paste
- 1 tablespoon lemon juice
  Salt and freshly ground pepper
- ¼ cup minced chives

1. In sauté pan melt butter. Add shrimp and sauté 1 minute. Add bourbon and set a match to it, shaking the pan until the flame dies down.

2. With slotted spoon remove shrimp to a warm platter. Add cream and tomato paste to pan. Bring mixture to a boil and reduce until it is thickened and coats the back of a spoon. Add lemon juice. Season to taste with salt and pepper.

3. Return shrimp to pan to reheat. Add chives just before serving.

Serves 4 to 6.

FISH IN CORIANDER SAUCE

This dish uses both the coriander seed and leaf (cilantro). Each has a completely different flavor. Serve with cooked black beans.

- 1½ pounds halibut, cut into serving-sized pieces
- 1 teaspoon salt
- ½ teaspoon freshly ground pepper
- ¼ cup unsalted butter
- 1 clove garlic, minced
- 1 small onion, peeled and chopped
- 1 tablespoon minced ginger
- 1½ teaspoons whole coriander seed, toasted
- ½ teaspoon turmeric
- ¾ cup Fish Fumet (page 17)
- 2 tablespoons lime juice
  Salt and freshly ground pepper to taste
- 1 cup cilantro leaves

1. Pat fish dry and sprinkle with the 1 teaspoon salt and the ½ teaspoon pepper. Heat butter in sauté pan and cook fish 2 to 4 minutes on each side; cooking time depends on thickness of fish. Remove fish to a warm platter.

2. To pan add garlic, onion, ginger, coriander seed, and turmeric. Stir and cook 2 to 3 minutes. Add fumet and simmer 3 minutes. Add lime juice; add fish and reheat in sauce.

3. Correct seasonings. Transfer to serving platter, and top with cilantro.

Serves 6 to 8.

PRAWNS WITH AMARETTO AND ALMONDS

Serve prawns with slices of toasted brioche and a glass of Champagne for a brunch or a midnight supper.

    8 *giant prawns, shelled and cleaned*
¼ *cup flour*
    3 *tablespoons unsalted butter*
¼ *cup white wine*
    2 *tablespoons amaretto*
    2 *tablespoons orange juice*
    2 *tablespoons almonds, toasted and skinned*

1. Cut prawns in half lengthwise. Sprinkle with flour.

2. In sauté pan heat butter. Add prawns and sauté until they begin to change color and curl. With slotted spoon, remove prawns to a warm plate.

3. Add wine, amaretto, and orange juice to pan. Sauté 30 seconds. Return prawns to pan, then heat gently. Sprinkle with almonds.

Serves 4 to 6.

FLOUNDER WITH MACADAMIA NUT SAUCE

This is a wonderfully rich dish. Serve with plain rice or Sweet-Potato Hash.

    6 *tablespoons clarified butter*
1½ *pounds flounder, cut in 6 pieces*
    1 *teaspoon salt*
½ *teaspoon freshly ground pepper*
    2 *cups whipping cream*
    3 *tablespoons lime juice*
¼ *cup unsalted butter*
½ *cup toasted, ground macadamia nuts*
      Salt and pepper to taste
    6 *slices lime (thin rounds) (for garnish)*
    2 *tablespoons toasted, ground macadamia nuts (for garnish)*

Sweet-Potato Hash

¼ *cup unsalted butter*
¼ *cup minced onion*
    2 *cups peeled, shredded sweet potatoes*
      Salt and freshly ground pepper to taste

1. In sauté pan heat the 6 tablespoons clarified butter. Add fish and sprinkle with the 1 teaspoon salt and ½ teaspoon pepper. Sauté until golden brown (5 to 6 minutes). With a slotted spoon, remove fish and place on warm platter. Pour fat from pan.

2. Add cream to pan, bring to a boil, and reduce to 1 cup. Add lime juice, reduce heat, and beat in the ¼ cup butter bit by bit. Add the ½ cup nuts. Correct seasonings.

3. Return fish to pan to reheat. Garnish with lime slices and the 2 tablespoons nuts.

Serves 6.

Sweet-Potato Hash In sauté pan melt butter. Add onion and potatoes and sauté until they begin to caramelize. Season to taste.

SOLE WITH ALMONDS, PINE NUTS, AND WHITE RAISINS

This is a variation of a Venetian dish called *sfogie in saor,* which means savory soles.

¼ *cup white raisins*
    2 *cups dry white wine*
    5 *tablespoons clarified butter*
¼ *cup slivered almonds*
    6 *sole fillets*
    1 *teaspoon salt*
½ *teaspoon freshly ground pepper*
    4 *tablespoons flour*
    3 *tablespoons unsalted butter*
    2 *tablespoons minced shallot*
      Salt and freshly ground pepper to taste
    2 *tablespoons pine nuts*

1. Soak raisins in white wine for 30 minutes. Remove raisins and reserve both wine and raisins.

2. In sauté pan heat the 5 tablespoons clarified butter. Add almonds to pan and sauté until they begin to color. Remove with slotted spoon and drain on paper towels.

3. Sprinkle fish with the 1 teaspoon salt, the ½ teaspoon pepper, and flour. Add fish to pan and sauté each side to a golden brown. Remove fish to a warm platter. Add the 3 tablespoons butter to pan. When butter has melted, add shallot and cook until soft. Add wine and raisins. Cook for 2 to 3 minutes and season to taste with salt and pepper. Add pine nuts to sauce and pour over fish.

Serves 6.

SHAD ROE SAUTÉ

Shad roe is only available in the spring and is usually sold in pairs (the term roe refers to a mass of eggs enclosed in a membrane, not an individual fish egg). The flavor is similar to a pâté. Serve with tiny new potatoes.

      Salt and freshly ground pepper
    2 *pairs shad roe*
      Flour for dredging
½ *cup clarified butter (see page 114)*
    2 *tablespoons dry white wine*
    2 *tablespoons chopped chives*
    1 *tablespoon minced parsley*
    1 *tablespoon lemon juice*
      Lemon wedges

1. Salt and pepper roe, then dredge in flour. Brush off excess.

2. In sauté pan heat butter. Add roe and sauté until golden brown (5 to 7 minutes per side). Remove to a warm platter.

3. Add wine to pan. Bring to a boil and reduce liquid slightly over high heat. Add chives, parsley, and lemon juice. Pour mixture over roe. Serve with lemon wedges.

Serves 2.

STIR-FRYING

Stir-frying is the Chinese equivalent of sautéing. Many of the basic principles are identical. Stir-frying requires higher temperatures, however, and, as a result, cooking times are shorter. The key to stir-frying is to keep the food moving constantly so that all parts of the ingredients come into contact with the hottest part of the cooking surface and cook quickly and evenly.

A wok is not a necessity, but the sloping sides make it much easier to toss the contents. Whatever pan you use should be large enough to permit rapid turning and tossing. Do not overload the wok; if it is crowded the hot oil will not sear each morsel and the juices will escape.

A successful stir-fry begins with food preparation. The ingredients must be cut into specific sizes to ensure rapid, uniform cooking. A marinade often coats the fish or shellfish with a seasoned mixture that adds flavor, seals in juices, and pre-

vents the absorption of the hot oil. As in a sauté, however, ingredients in a stir-fry are not always coated.

Stir-frying uses vegetable oil. Peanut oil and corn oil are the most common. Some cooks add ginger or garlic to the hot oil to flavor it before the cooking begins.

Because stir-frying is such a rapid process, organization is extremely important. All the utensils should be within reach. All the ingredients and condiments should be prepared and ready. A successful stir-fry allows no time for hesitation. The cook adds the ingredients in steps, first the ingredients that require longer cooking time, then the more fragile components. Be aware of a crucial distinction: In this case "stirring" does not mean a flat, circular motion. A stir-fry requires tossing, turning, and flipping to keep food moving rapidly. Always serve a stir-fry immediately.

The tastes of toasty nuts and sweet raisins offer an interesting contrast to the mild-flavored fish in Sole With Almonds, Pine Nuts, and White Raisins. Sauté the nuts in clarified butter to bring out their flavor.

PRAWNS WITH CHUTNEY

The Chinese, inventors of the wok, never use butter; the Japanese, who do not use a wok, use butter occasionally. Serve this culture-spanning dish with rice.

¾ cup chutney
½ cup water
3 tablespoons Japanese vinegar
6 tablespoons clarified butter (see page 114)
1 clove garlic, minced
2 tablespoons minced ginger
2 small dried red chiles, seeded, and minced
1½ pounds medium prawns, shelled and deveined
2 tablespoons toasted sesame seed
¾ cup slivered green onion (3-inch strips)

1. Chop the chunks of chutney into smaller pieces. Combine chutney, water, and vinegar; set aside. Heat butter in a wok, then add garlic and ginger. Stir-fry for 30 seconds. Add chiles and toss.

2. Add prawns and stir-fry until they turn pink. Remove prawns from wok with a slotted spoon and keep warm.

3. Add chutney mixture to wok. Bring to a boil and reduce mixture over high heat, until it thickens slightly. Return prawns to sauce and heat.

4. Arrange prawns on a platter and sprinkle with sesame seed and onion.

Serves 6 to 8.

HOT-AND-SOUR SHARK

Shark is a wonderfully full-flavored and versatile fish that lends itself to many types of cooking. The technique of coating and partially cooking the fish is called velveting and is common in Chinese cuisine. Serve with steamed rice.

2 cups water
  Zest of 1 orange, julienned (use orange part of rind only)
2 egg whites
2 tablespoons dry sherry
3 tablespoons cornstarch
4 tablespoons peanut oil
1 teaspoon salt
1 pound shark, cut in 1- by ½-inch cubes
  Oil, for deep-frying
½ cup orange juice
½ cup chicken stock
4 tablespoons rice vinegar
2 tablespoons sugar
2 tablespoons soy sauce
½ cup julienned ginger (2-inch strips)
2 dried red chiles, seeded and minced
½ cup slivered green onion (3-inch strips)
1 cup seeded, julienned red bell pepper
2 tablespoons minced green onion

1. Bring the water to a boil. Add the orange zest and boil 1 minute. Remove zest with slotted spoon, drain, and reserve.

2. Combine egg whites, sherry, 2 tablespoons of the cornstarch, 2 tablespoons of the peanut oil, and salt. Add shark pieces to mixture and coat well.

3. In a large pot heat oil for deep-frying to 350° F. Add shark pieces and fry until golden brown, 2 to 3 minutes. Remove shark and drain on paper towels. Keep warm.

4. In small bowl combine orange juice, chicken stock, vinegar, remaining 1 tablespoon cornstarch, sugar, and soy sauce. In wok heat remaining 2 tablespoons peanut oil. Add ginger and chiles; stir-fry 1 minute. Add the ½ cup slivered green onion and bell pepper; stir-fry 1 minute. Add orange juice mixture; stir until it thickens.

5. Return shark to wok, add zest, toss, and reheat. Garnish with the 2 tablespoons minced green onion and serve immediately.

Serves 4 to 6.

STIR-FRIED OYSTERS

These oysters are wonderful served with buckwheat noodles from a Japanese food store.

1 tablespoon cornstarch
1 tablespoon water
2 cups water
  Zest of 1 orange, julienned (use orange part of rind only)
3 tablespoons peanut oil
1 clove garlic, minced
2 tablespoons minced green onion
1 tablespoon minced peeled ginger
¾ pound small oysters, drained
⅓ cup orange juice
3 tablespoons soy sauce

1. Combine cornstarch and the 1 tablespoon water. Set aside.

2. Bring the 2 cups water to a boil. Add the orange zest and blanch for 1 minute. Remove zest with a slotted spoon and reserve.

3. Heat oil in wok. Add garlic, onion, and ginger. Stir-fry for 1 minute. Add oysters, orange juice, and soy sauce. Stir-fry for 30 seconds. Add cornstarch mixture and zest. Cook until sauce thickens (30 seconds to 1 minute). Serve immediately.

Serves 4.

FOUR-TREASURE RICE

Serve this dish with a salad for a light lunch or as an accompaniment to other fish dishes. The lack of soy sauce gives this rice a delicate flavor.

6 tablespoons peanut oil
1 teaspoon salt
4 cups cooked long-grain rice, cooled
¾ cup finely chopped onion
1½ cups bay shrimp or pieces of cooked shrimp
1 cup crab claw meat
¼ cup peas
½ cup green onion, slivered (2-inch strips)
3 eggs
¾ teaspoon salt

1. In wok heat 4 tablespoons of the oil. Add the 1 teaspoon salt, then add rice, breaking up any clumps. Toss until rice is well coated with oil and stir-fry for 2 minutes.

2. Add the ¾ cup chopped onion, shrimp, crab, peas, and the slivered green onions. Toss and heat through.

3. In a small pan heat the remaining 2 tablespoons oil. Add eggs and the ¾ teaspoon salt. Scramble lightly. When curds begin to form, add eggs to rice and toss together. Correct seasonings. Serve immediately.

Serves 6 to 8.

CURRIED SCALLOPS

Bay and sea scallops are very different in size, so cooking times vary. Serve with steamed rice.

¾ pound scallops (if large, cut in half)
¾ teaspoon salt
½ teaspoon freshly ground pepper
4 tablespoons peanut oil
1 clove garlic
¼ cup minced onion
1 tablespoon curry powder
½ cup chicken stock

½ cup peas
½ cup slivered green onion (cut in diagonal slivers ¼ inch long)
1 tablespoon cornstarch (optional)
2 tablespoons water (optional) Salt and freshly ground pepper to taste

1. Pat scallops dry, sprinkle with the ¾ teaspoon salt and the ½ teaspoon pepper. Heat 2 tablespoons of the oil in wok and stir-fry scallops 1½ to 3 minutes, depending on their size. Remove scallops from wok.

2. Add the remaining 2 tablespoons peanut oil to wok and heat. Add garlic and the ¼ cup minced onion. Stir-fry for 30 seconds. Add curry powder, toss, then add chicken stock. Bring to a boil and reduce by a third.

3. Add peas and green onion. Toss constantly for 1 minute. Add scallops and reheat. If sauce is thin, mix cornstarch with water and add to sauce. Season with salt and pepper.

Serves 4.

A quick and easy entrée, Curried Scallops fit neatly into the requirements for a time-saving special meal. A good curry powder is essential to the success of this recipe.

DEEP-FRYING

Fried foods have a reputation for being heavy, greasy, and fattening; however, when food is fried correctly, it absorbs only a small amount of fat.

The best fats for deep-frying are peanut oil, corn oil, and solid vegetable shortening. The temperature of this fat is the most important factor in deep-frying. If it is too cold, the food will absorb the fat. If it is too hot, the outside of the food will burn before the inside cooks.

It is oil that has been burned or that has been reused too many times that makes many fried foods objectionable. Fat that has not been burned may be carefully strained through a damp cheesecloth and used several times. Once oil has been used for cooking fish, however, do not use it to cook any other type of food because the fish flavors the oil.

The best temperature for deep-frying is 375° F. Use a deep-fry thermometer to check the temperature. You can also throw a small cube of bread into the oil; if the oil is at the correct temperature, the bread browns in 30 seconds. Or you can just look at the oil. If a haze is apparent, the oil is about 375° F. If blue smoke appears, however, the temperature is over 400° F and the oil is burning. Reduce the heat immediately.

The rate at which you add fish to hot oil is also important. Adding too many fish at one time lowers the temperature dramatically. Allow the fat to reheat between batches so that the hot oil immediately seals the surface of the raw food.

Since the heat of deep-frying is intense, the type of coating is a prime consideration. Batter that is thick enough to coat evenly and prevent drying is effective. The skins of small whole fish work as a protective coating; a light dusting of flour or cornmeal is sufficient for them.

When deep-frying, use a heavy pan, and fill it only halfway with oil so the oil won't boil over when you add fish. To keep from overcooking the outside and undercooking the inside, use fish that is less than 2 inches thick.

Use tongs or a slotted spoon to handle fried foods; don't pierce them with a fork. Place fried fish on paper towels to drain any excess fat, then place fish in a warm oven until all the fish is ready to serve.

SALT COD FRITTERS

Salt cod has a flavor that can become addictive. These fritters make wonderful appetizers. Make the purée ahead of time and deep-fry at the last minute. Serve with Aïoli (page 118).

    1 pound salt cod
    ½ cup finely chopped
        green onion
    ¼ cup minced Italian parsley
    2 medium shallots, minced
    ¼ teaspoon freshly
        grated nutmeg
    ⅛ teaspoon freshly
        ground pepper
    1 cup flour
    1½ cups milk
        Oil, for deep-frying

1. Cover the cod with water and soak for 24 hours, changing the water several times to reduce saltiness.

2. Drain cod, then place in a pan with fresh cold water to cover. Bring to a boil, then simmer until the cod begins to flake (20 to 30 minutes). Drain and cool.

3. In food processor fitted with steel blade, purée the cod, onion, parsley, shallot, nutmeg, and pepper. In a small bowl combine flour and milk. With machine running, add milk mixture to puréed cod.

4. Transfer mixture to a bowl, cover, and let rest for 1½ to 2 hours.

5. Using two tablespoons as a mold, form the batter into 1-inch balls. In a large pot heat oil to 350° F to 375° F. Deep-fry fritters until golden brown (2 to 3 minutes). Drain and serve as soon as possible.

Makes 30 fritters.

FISH AND CHIPS

Fish and chips are to the British what hamburgers are to Americans. Although you may find different species of fish at the fish-and-chips stand, the cooking method is the same for all and all receive a sprinkle of malt vinegar.

    ¾ cup flour
    1 egg yolk
    4 tablespoons beer
    4 tablespoons water
    ½ teaspoon salt
    1 egg white
        Oil, for deep-frying
    1 pound haddock,
        boned, skinned, and cut in
        3- by 5-inch pieces

Chips

    Potatoes

1. Put flour in a medium bowl. In another medium bowl, combine yolk, beer, water, and salt. Pour liquid into flour, whisking until smooth. Allow to rest for 30 minutes.

2. Beat egg white to soft peaks, then fold into batter.

3. In a large pot heat oil to 375° F. Dip fish into batter, then deep-fry until golden brown (4 to 5 minutes). Drain.

Makes 30 pieces.

Chips Cut potatoes into ½-inch strips. Deep-fry in the same oil used for the fish.

Fish and Chips are a favorite on both sides of the Atlantic. For authenticity, the malt vinegar is a must . . . the newspaper wrapping is just an option.

Fritto Misto With Caper Mayonnaise uses a combination of fish and shellfish, allowing the cook to select seasonal favorites.

FRITTO MISTO WITH CAPER MAYONNAISE

A traditional Christmas Eve food in Italian homes, fritto misto often includes eel and cod. The term means mixed fry, so use any combination of fish and shellfish that appeals to you. Serve as part of a buffet with an assortment of salads.

>   2 cups flour
>   2 teaspoons fresh rosemary
>   or 1 teaspoon dried
> 1¼ teaspoons salt
>   2 tablespoons dry sherry
>   2 tablespoons oil
> 1½ cups water
>   1 pound squid, cleaned
>   12 small smelt
>   ½ pound angler, cut in
>   ¼-inch medallions
>   1 pound shrimp, cleaned
>   Salt and freshly ground
>   pepper
>   4 to 6 tablespoons lemon juice
>   Oil, for deep-frying
>   Lemon wedges (optional)

Caper Mayonnaise

>   1 cup Basic Mayonnaise
>   (see page 117)
>   3 tablespoons lemon juice
>   ¼ cup capers, drained

1. Combine flour, rosemary, and the 1¼ teaspoons salt. Add sherry and 2 tablespoons oil to the water. Beat water mixture into flour mixture until smooth. Cover and let rest 1 hour.

2. Cut the bodies of squid into 1-inch circles. Leave the tentacles whole. Lay cleaned squid, smelt, angler, and shrimp on a platter. Sprinkle with salt, pepper, and lemon juice. Let stand for 5 minutes, then pat dry.

3. In a large pot heat oil to 375° F. Dip fish and shellfish into batter. Deep-fry a few pieces at a time. Drain on paper towels. Place in a warm (200° F) oven until all are fried.

4. Serve with lemon wedges or Caper Mayonnaise.

Serves 8 to 10.

Caper Mayonnaise Whisk together all ingredients, mixing well.

HAWAIIAN SHRIMP GEORGE

The sweetness of the shrimp and pineapple provide an interesting contrast to the piquant tomato chutney. For an entrée, serve chutney on the side. For a party, place the sauce in the middle of a platter and mound the shrimp around it.

>   ½ cup flour
>   ⅛ teaspoon cayenne pepper
>   1 teaspoon salt
>   ¾ teaspoon ground ginger
>   24 jumbo shrimp, shelled and
>   deveined (leave tails on
>   if possible)
>   2 eggs
>   1 tablespoon water
>   7 ounces shredded coconut
>   Oil, for deep-frying
>   ½ cup crushed pineapple

Tomato Chutney

>   2 pounds ripe tomatoes,
>   peeled, seeded, and chopped
> 1½ cups sugar
>   1 clove garlic, minced
>   1 teaspoon salt
>   1 teaspoon crushed dried
>   red pepper
>   2 teaspoons ground ginger
>   1 cup cider vinegar

1. Combine flour, cayenne, salt, and ginger. Dust shrimp with this mixture.

2. Beat eggs with the water. Dip floured shrimp into eggs, then roll shrimp in coconut.

3. In a large pot heat oil to 350° F. Deep-fry shrimp in hot oil until coconut browns. Drain on paper towels.

4. Combine pineapple and 1¼ cups Tomato Chutney to serve as a sauce for shrimp.

Serves 6 to 8 as an entrée.

Tomato Chutney In a saucepan combine all ingredients. Cook, uncovered, over very low heat, stirring occasionally, until thick (about 45 minutes).

CLAM, CORN, AND CHILE FRITTERS

These delicious fried bits of food, often used as an appetizer, are almost always dipped in a sauce (see page 114) or mayonnaise flavored with clam juice, and accompanied with lemon wedges.

>   3 eggs
>   1 cup minced clams
>   ½ cup cracker crumbs
>   1 cup corn kernels
>   1 teaspoon minced
>   jalapeño pepper
>   1 teaspoon salt
>   ½ teaspoon pepper
>   Clam juice to moisten
>   (optional)
>   Oil, for deep-frying

1. In a medium bowl beat eggs. Add clams, cracker crumbs, corn, jalapeño peppers, salt, and pepper. If mixture is too dry, add clam juice to make a thick batter.

2. In a large pot heat oil to 375° F. Using two tablespoons as a mold, create mounds of batter and drop them into hot oil. Fry until golden brown, about 5 minutes. Remove fritters with a slotted spoon, drain on paper towels, then serve.

Makes about 18 fritters.

SKATE BEIGNETS

Because skate feed primarily on shell-fish, they have a wonderful, delicate flavor. Only the wings of the skate are edible, and you eat them the same way that you eat an artichoke. Serve with lemon wedges along with a delicately flavored green or vegetable salad.

- 1 cup flour
- 1 teaspoon baking powder
- ½ teaspoon salt
- 1 egg
- 1 cup milk
- 2 tablespoons oil
- 2 pounds skate wings, cut in strips
  Oil, for deep-frying
  Flour, for dredging

1. In a medium bowl sift together the 1 cup flour, baking powder, and salt. In a small bowl mix together the egg, milk, and the 2 tablespoons oil. Add the liquid ingredients to the flour mixture. Mix well.

2. In a large pot heat oil to 375° F. Dip skate pieces into batter, then into flour. Deep-fry in hot oil until golden brown (about 5 minutes).

Serves 6 to 8.

MISSISSIPPI FRIED SHRIMP

A southern speciality, these fried shrimp are served in heavily buttered, hollowed-out loaves of hot bread. Accompany with steamed ears of corn or sliced tomatoes.

- 1 cup Basic Mayonnaise (see page 117)
- 1 tablespoon lemon juice
- 1 teaspoon Dijon mustard
- 2 to 5 dashes hot-pepper sauce
- 1 pound shrimp, shelled and deveined
- 2 cups soft, fresh bread crumbs
- 1 cup clarified butter (see page 114)

1. Combine mayonnaise, lemon juice, mustard, and hot-pepper sauce.

2. Dip shrimp in mayonnaise, then in bread crumbs.

3. Melt butter. Fry shrimp in butter until crisp (2 to 3 minutes).

Serves 4 to 6.

CATFISH AND BLACK WALNUTS ON GREENS

Black walnuts have a definite, almost fermented taste, which provides a complementary contrast to the sweet catfish. Accompany with baked toma-toes and crusty bread.

- 2 egg whites
- 6 tablespoons cornstarch
- 2 teaspoons salt
- 2 tablespoons bourbon
- ½ teaspoon freshly ground pepper
- 1 pound catfish, skinned, boned, and cut in 1-inch pieces
  Oil, for deep-frying
- 1 cup finely chopped black walnuts

Greens

- 2 tablespoons bacon fat
- 2 bunches dandelion greens
- 1 to 3 tablespoons malt vinegar
  Salt and freshly ground pepper to taste

1. Combine egg whites, cornstarch, salt, bourbon, and pepper. Add catfish to mixture, coating each piece well. Cover and marinate fish in refrigera-tor for 45 minutes.

2. In a large pot heat oil to 375° F. Dip each piece of catfish in nuts and deep-fry in hot oil until golden brown (about 5 minutes). Remove fish with slotted spoon and drain on paper towels.

3. Place on bed of sautéed greens and serve immediately.

Serves 4 to 6.

Greens In a large sauté pan melt bacon fat. Add greens. Sauté over medium heat until greens start to wilt. Add malt vinegar. Season with salt and pepper. Remove from heat.

Dandelion greens and bourbon are just two of the unusual ingredients that combine in this recipe for Catfish and Black Walnuts on Greens.

*Caviar connotes extravagance,
but in fact a little goes a
long way. Use it in dishes
ranging from simple appetizers
to sophisticated sauces.*

Entertaining

This chapter contains recipes—contributed by talented cooks and chefs from throughout the country—for appetizers, caviar, sushi, and entrées, including some main dish salads. You'll also find an extensive selection of delicious sauces; the same fish can take on a completely different look and taste just by a change of sauce, providing many options for entertaining. Your individual creativity can truly shine when you use fish and shellfish for your festive occasions. Experiment and enjoy!

APPETIZERS

Appetizers used to be associated with formal cocktail parties. Today they are also referred to as hors d'oeuvres and are served at casual gatherings, tailgate parties, lunches, or even afternoon tea. They can be as simple or as sophisticated as the cook desires. The variety of recipes here reflects this range.

DEVILED CRAB

This East Coast favorite is a wonderful appetizer. With the addition of a crisp green salad, it would serve as a light supper dish.

- ¼ cup unsalted butter
- ½ cup chopped green bell pepper
- ½ cup chopped onion
- ¼ cup chopped celery
  Kosher salt and freshly ground pepper to taste
- 1 teaspoon dried tarragon
- 1 tablespoon Worcestershire sauce
  Dash hot-pepper sauce
- 1 teaspoon dry mustard
- 6 tablespoons flour
- 2 cups milk
- 2 pounds cooked crabmeat
- 2 tablespoons minced pimiento
- ½ cup dried bread crumbs
- 2 tablespoons unsalted butter
  Toast points

1. Preheat broiler. Melt the ¼ cup butter in a large skillet. Add green pepper, onion, celery, salt, pepper, tarragon, Worcestershire, hot-pepper sauce, and mustard. Cook over low heat until vegetables soften. Add flour and mix well. Add milk and cook until mixture thickens, stirring constantly.

2. Add crab and pimiento; mix well. Sprinkle bread crumbs over crab mixture, then dot with the 2 tablespoons butter. Broil until crumbs are lightly browned. Serve with toast points.

Serves 6 to 8.

SHRIMP AND CASHEW SAMOSAS

Diane Gould is a graduate of Tante Marie's Cooking School in San Francisco. She has worked as a caterer and as an assistant to various chefs. She also develops recipes, and this recipe is an example of her talents.

- 2 tablespoons peanut oil
- 1 teaspoon black mustard seed
- ½ pound shrimp, shelled, deveined, and coarsely chopped
- ½ cup toasted cashews, coarsely chopped
- ⅓ cup frozen peas, thawed
- ⅓ cup shredded carrot
- 1 small red potato, cooked, peeled, and cubed
- 3 tablespoons chopped cilantro
- 3 cloves garlic, minced
- 2 teaspoons minced peeled fresh ginger
- ¾ cup chopped onion
- 1 teaspoon salt
- ½ teaspoon ground coriander
- ¼ teaspoon turmeric
- ⅛ teaspoon cayenne pepper, or to taste
  Vegetable oil, for frying
  Cilantro Chutney (page 121)

Samosa Dough

- 2 cups flour
- 1 teaspoon salt
- ¼ cup butter, melted and cooled
- ½ to ¾ cup water

1. Heat the 2 tablespoons peanut oil in a 9-inch skillet. Add mustard seed and cook until they begin to pop. Add shrimp; cook until they turn pink (1 to 2 minutes).

2. Add cashews, peas, carrot, potato, cilantro, garlic, ginger, and onion. Sauté this mixture 2 to 3 minutes over medium heat. Add salt, coriander, turmeric, and cayenne, and cook 2 to 3 minutes more. Set aside to cool.

3. Prepare Samosa Dough. Place a heaping teaspoon of shrimp mixture on one side of each piece of dough. Moisten edge of dough with water and fold the unfilled half over the filling. Pinch edges together to seal.

4. Heat 2 inches vegetable oil in a wok or heavy pan. Deep-fry three samosas at a time until they turn golden brown. Drain on paper towels and serve warm with Cilantro Chutney.

Makes 40 samosas.

Samosa Dough In a food processor or medium bowl of electric mixer, combine flour and salt. Mix well. Cut butter into flour mixture. With machine running, add enough water in a steady, slow stream so the flour mixture forms a ball. Roll dough into a cylinder on a lightly floured board and divide into 10 equal pieces. Roll each piece into an 8-inch circle, and cut each circle into quarters.

POTTED PECAN SHRIMP

Serve this potted shrimp with crackers or raw vegetables. It may be made a few days ahead if covered and refrigerated.

- 8 ounces cream cheese
- 2 tablespoons minced celery
- 2 teaspoons grated onion
- 2 tablespoons beer
- ¼ teaspoon Worcestershire sauce
- ⅛ teaspoon dry mustard
- ½ cup cooked, chopped shrimp meat
- ½ cup toasted, chopped pecans

In a medium bowl mix cream cheese, celery, onion, beer, Worcestershire, and mustard. Stir in shrimp and pecans. Pack into serving container and chill.

Serves 8 to 10.

Showing off the versatility of crab and shrimp (top to bottom): Potted Pecan Shrimp, Deviled Crab with black bread, and Shrimp and Cashew Samosas.

A variation on Smoked Salmon Pie, these small tarts are garnished with red salmon roe and dill. This recipe can be used to make small tartlets, as shown, or a whole pie as described in the recipe on the facing page.

MUSSELS WITH BLACK WALNUT SAUCE

If black walnuts are unavailable, you may substitute another variety, though the flavor will be different.

- 24 large mussels
- ¼ cup black walnuts
- ¼ cup soft bread crumbs
- ½ cup olive oil
- 2 teaspoons red wine vinegar
- 1 teaspoon balsamic vinegar
  Dash hot-pepper sauce
  Kosher salt and freshly ground pepper to taste

1. Clean and steam mussels until they open. Cool, then remove and discard top shells. Mussels will be served in the bottom shell.

2. To prepare sauce, in food processor fitted with steel blade, place walnuts, bread crumbs, oil, red wine vinegar, balsamic vinegar, hot-pepper sauce, salt, and pepper. Blend until smooth.

3. Spoon sauce over each mussel. Cover and chill for 1 hour.

Makes 2 dozen appetizers.

ENGLISH POTTED KIPPERS

Served as pub food in England, potted kippers are a terrific addition to any party table. Serve with toast.

    1 pound kippered herring
    ½ cup unsalted butter
    2 tablespoons lemon juice
      Dash hot-pepper sauce
      Freshly ground black pepper

1. Place herring in a medium bowl. Pour boiling water over herring to cover; let stand for about 5 minutes. Drain kippers and pat dry with paper towels. Remove skin and bones.

2. In a food processor fitted with steel blade, process kippers, butter, lemon juice, hot-pepper sauce, and pepper until smooth. Chill and serve.

Makes 2 cups.

SMOKED SALMON PIE

Prebake a pie shell to reduce preparation time on serving day. This easy appetizer also makes a great supper.

    2 tablespoons unsalted butter
    ¾ cup chopped green onion
    6 ounces smoked salmon,
      chopped
      Kosher salt and freshly
      ground black pepper to taste
      Dash cayenne pepper, or
      to taste
    ½ pound ricotta cheese
    2 large eggs, lightly beaten
      9-inch baked pastry shell

1. Preheat oven to 350° F. Melt butter in a medium skillet. Add onion and sauté until soft. Stir in salmon, salt, pepper, and cayenne.

2. Mix cheese with beaten eggs, then pour into baked pie shell. Spoon salmon mixture over cheese mixture and spread evenly.

3. Bake until set, 45 to 50 minutes. Let stand 5 minutes before serving.

Serves 6 to 8.

HERRING MOUSSE

Here is a make-ahead mousse that serves a large crowd. Even guests who do not usually like fish enjoy this party favorite. Serve with crackers.

    1 tablespoon unflavored gelatin
      (1 envelope)
    ¾ cup half-and-half
    1 jar (12 oz) herring fillets
      in sour cream
    1 jar (2 oz) pimiento strips
    2 teaspoons Dijon mustard
    2 teaspoons prepared
      horseradish
    ⅓ cup thinly sliced green onion
    ¼ cup chopped pimiento-stuffed
      green olives
    1 cup sour cream
    ½ cup Basic Mayonnaise (see
      page 117)
    1 tablespoon lemon juice

1. Sprinkle gelatin over half-and-half in a small bowl. Let stand 5 minutes to soften. Set over boiling water and heat until gelatin dissolves. Cool to room temperature.

2. Reserving two pieces of herring for garnish, place herring in a food processor fitted with a steel blade. Process until smooth. Add cool gelatin mixture and process until well blended.

3. Transfer to a large bowl and stir in pimiento, mustard, horseradish, onion, and olives. Fold in sour cream, mayonnaise, and lemon juice. Turn into an oiled 6-cup mold. Chill overnight or until firm. To serve, unmold and garnish with reserved herring.

Serves 10 to 12.

CLAM PUFFS

These miniature soufflés are delicious and make a stunning presentation.

    1 dozen clams
    ¼ cup unsalted butter
    ½ cup chopped green onion
      (include part of the green)
    ½ pound chopped fresh
      mushrooms
    1 cup chopped prosciutto
    ½ teaspoon Dijon mustard
    3 tablespoons flour
      Kosher salt and freshly
      ground pepper to taste
    7 egg whites, beaten to
      stiff peaks

1. Preheat oven to 400° F. Wash and shuck clams and chop, reserving shells. In a medium skillet melt butter. Add onions and mushrooms, and sauté until soft.

2. Add clams, prosciutto, mustard, flour, salt, and pepper. Stirring constantly, cook until thick. Spoon into greased clam shells and cover with beaten egg whites.

3. Bake until lightly browned, about 10 minutes.

Makes 2 dozen puffs.

PRAWNS WITH CILANTRO CHUTNEY

If outdoor entertaining is your style, these prawns may be grilled. Whether outdoors or indoors, use wooden skewers that have been soaked in water for 1 hour.

    ⅓ cup olive oil
    2 cloves garlic, minced
    1 pound large prawns, shelled
      and deveined (leave tails
      attached)
      Cilantro Chutney (see
      page 121)

1. In a medium bowl combine olive oil and garlic. Add prawns and marinate for at least 1 hour.

2. Preheat broiler. Thread 3 or 4 prawns on each skewer and broil until pink. Serve with chutney.

Serves 4.

APPLE-SHRIMP APPETIZERS

A boon to the busy cook, Apple-Shrimp Appetizers can be made ahead and frozen. To prevent the filo dough from drying out while preparing the filling, work quickly, and keep these ultra-thin sheets of pastry covered with a damp dish towel.

 2 tablespoons vegetable oil
 1 medium onion, chopped
 1 apple, peeled and shredded
 2 teaspoons curry powder
 1 teaspoon salt
 1 pound cooked bay shrimp
 1 medium potato, cooked, peeled, and mashed
 1 pound filo dough
 1 cup melted clarified butter (see page 114)

1. Preheat oven to 350° F. Heat oil in a medium skillet. Add onion and apple; cook until soft. Mix in curry powder and salt, then remove from heat.

2. In a medium bowl combine shrimp, potato, and onion mixture. Chill thoroughly.

3. Brush 1 sheet of filo with some of the melted butter. Fold into thirds lengthwise to form a 4-inch-wide strip. Place a heaping tablespoon of shrimp mixture in bottom corner of strip. Fold strip like a flag to form a triangle. Place on ungreased baking sheet. Brush triangle with melted butter.

4. Repeat process until filo and filling are used. Bake until golden brown, about 20 minutes.

Makes 20 to 25 triangles.

CRAB-STUFFED SHRIMP

The combination of crab and shrimp is a universal favorite. This attractive presentation could be the center of a buffet table.

 24 large shrimp
  2 cups cooked crabmeat
 1/3 cup Basic Mayonnaise (see page 117)
  2 teaspoons minced chives
 1/4 teaspoon curry powder
  1 teaspoon lemon juice
    Kosher salt and freshly ground pepper to taste

1. Poach shrimp until done, 2 to 3 minutes. Drain and cool. Shell shrimp, leaving tails intact. Make a deep slit in the back of each shrimp and remove vein.

2. In a medium bowl combine crabmeat, mayonnaise, chives, curry powder, lemon juice, salt, and pepper.

3. Stuff shrimp with crab mixture and arrange on platter.

Makes 2 dozen stuffed shrimp.

CRAB CAKES

With the addition of chopped hot peppers, this typical East Coast recipe becomes a Gulf Coast favorite.

 1/4 cup unsalted butter
 1/3 cup chopped onion
 2/3 cup soft bread crumbs
  2 eggs, lightly beaten
  1 teaspoon Dijon mustard
  1 tablespoon minced parsley
    Kosher salt and freshly ground pepper to taste
 1½ cups cooked crabmeat
  2 cups soft bread crumbs
 ½ cup clarified butter (see page 114)

1. In a small skillet melt butter and sauté onion until soft. Place cooked onion in a medium bowl and add the 2/3 cup bread crumbs, eggs, mustard, parsley, salt, and pepper; mix well.

2. Add crabmeat and mix well. Drop heaping tablespoons of mixture into the 2 cups bread crumbs to coat. Melt clarified butter in a medium skillet, and cook the crab cakes over medium-high heat until golden brown, about 2 minutes on each side. Drain on paper towels and serve.

Makes 12 to 14 cakes.

TAPENADE

This dish from the French region of Provence used to be extremely time-consuming because the ingredients needed to be pounded. Now, with the food processor, tapenade takes only minutes to prepare. Serve with toast or crisp crackers.

 1½ cups French oil-cured black olives
 1/3 cup olive oil
  3 tablespoons lemon juice
  2 tablespoons Cognac
  1 can (6½ oz) oil-packed tuna fish
 1/4 cup capers, drained
  2 ounces oil-packed anchovy fillets
  2 cloves garlic, minced
  2 teaspoons Dijon mustard
 ½ teaspoon freshly ground pepper
    Pinch ground cloves
    Pinch ground ginger
    Pinch ground nutmeg

In food processor fitted with steel blade, process olives with olive oil. Add lemon juice, Cognac, tuna, capers, anchovies, garlic, mustard, pepper, cloves, ginger, and nutmeg. Process to a smooth paste.

Makes 1½ cups.

SALMON CHEESE GÂTEAU

Surround this cheese dish with red and green apple slices. The cake itself may be made a few days in advance.

- ¼ pound Camembert
- ¼ pound Gruyère, finely grated
- ¼ pound blue cheese
- 1½ pounds cream cheese
- 3 tablespoons Lemon Crème Fraîche (see page 119) or sour cream
- ½ pound smoked salmon, chopped
- ½ pound pecans, toasted and chopped

1. Line a 10-inch quiche pan with plastic wrap. In a medium bowl mix Camembert, Gruyère, blue cheese, and 1 pound of the cream cheese. Set aside. Mix remaining ½ pound cream cheese with Lemon Crème Fraîche.

2. Spread crème fraîche mixture over bottom of lined quiche pan. Sprinkle with salmon and pecans.

3. Cover salmon and nuts with Camembert mixture. Completely cover with plastic wrap and refrigerate at least 4 to 5 hours. To serve, remove top plastic wrap, turn onto platter, and pull away remaining wrap.

Serves 10 to 12.

CRAB AND ENDIVE WITH POTATOES CAVIAR

This combination is a visual treat—the long, elegant endive leaves complement the round potatoes. Use whatever kind of caviar you like best.

- 1 cup crabmeat
- ¼ cup Basic Mayonnaise (see page 117)
- 2 teaspoons curry powder
- 2 tablespoons chopped water chestnuts
  Freshly ground white pepper to taste
- 2 to 4 stalks endive (amount depends on size)
- 12 tiny new potatoes
- ½ cup Lemon Crème Fraîche (see page 119) or sour cream
  Black, red, or golden caviar

1. In a small bowl combine crab, mayonnaise, curry powder, water chestnuts, and pepper. Cut root end from endive so the leaves separate. Place 1 heaping teaspoon of crab mixture on the root end of each leaf.

2. In a medium pan filled with salted water, boil potatoes until tender. Drain and let cool. Cut potatoes in half, and with melon baller scoop out some of the center of each half. Fill each cavity with Lemon Crème Fraîche and top with caviar.

3. Arrange the endive leaves on a platter in a spoke pattern. Between each leaf place a caviar potato. Serve at room temperature.

Makes 2 dozen appetizers.

Crab and Endive With Potatoes Caviar makes an attractive presentation for a party. The crab mixture and potatoes may be made ahead and the dish quickly assembled just before guests arrive.

Use a pastry bag with a large star tip to fill Salmon Cucumber Cups with herbed cheese. A caper and a sprig of dill complement the taste of the cheese and add visual interest.

TARAMASALATA

Serve this Greek appetizer as a spread or a dip. Often called caviar spread, it is actually made with salted carp roe, which Greek specialty stores usually sell.

> Two 1-inch-thick slices firm white bread
> ¼ cup tarama (carp roe)
> 3 tablespoons lemon juice
> ½ cup olive oil
> 2 tablespoons chopped onion
> Chopped Italian parsley (for garnish)

1. Trim crusts from bread. Soak bread slices in cold water briefly and squeeze dry.

2. In a food processor fitted with steel blade, combine bread, tarama, lemon juice, 2 tablespoons olive oil, and the onion. Process and gradually add remaining oil, until the mixture resembles mayonnaise. Chill thoroughly. Garnish with parsley and serve.

Makes 1 to 1½ cups.

SMOKED OYSTER DIP

    8 ounces cream cheese
    1 can smoked oysters
    ½ cup chopped ripe olives
    ½ cup Basic Mayonnaise
       (see page 117)
    2 teaspoons lemon juice
       Dash hot-pepper sauce

Let cream cheese warm to room temperature. Drain and chop oysters. Combine cream cheese, oysters, olives, mayonnaise, lemon juice, and hot-pepper sauce. Serve with crackers.

Makes 1½ cups.

SHRIMP ROUNDS

    ½ pound small bay shrimp,
       cooked
    ¼ to ⅓ cup Basic Mayonnaise
       (see page 117)
    1 teaspoon dried dill weed
       Kosher salt and freshly
       ground white pepper to taste
    1 English (hothouse) cucumber

1. Gently mix shrimp, mayonnaise, dill, salt, and pepper. Set aside for 30 minutes to blend flavors.

2. Slice cucumber into ¼-inch rounds. Place a heaping spoonful of shrimp mixture on each round and serve.

Makes 2 dozen appetizers.

ARTICHOKE SPREAD

    1 cup sour cream or Lemon
       Crème Fraîche (see page 119)
    8 ounces cream cheese, at
       room temperature
    ½ cup chopped artichoke hearts
    1 jar (2 oz) black
       lumpfish caviar

In small bowl mix sour cream and cream cheese until well blended. Mix in artichoke hearts. Gently fold in caviar. Serve with raw vegetables or crackers.

Makes 2 cups.

SALMON BALL

    1 can (1 lb) red salmon
    8 ounces cream cheese, at
       room temperature
    1 tablespoon lemon juice
    1 tablespoon minced onion
    1 teaspoon prepared horseradish
    ¼ teaspoon salt
    ½ teaspoon liquid smoke
    ⅓ cup roasted chopped pecans
    ¼ cup chopped parsley

1. Drain salmon; remove bones and skin. In a medium bowl mix cream cheese, lemon juice, onion, horseradish, salt, and liquid smoke. Add salmon, mix well and form into a ball. Chill overnight.

2. Combine pecans and parsley. Roll salmon ball in nut mixture. Serve with crisp crackers.

Serves 12.

SALMON CUCUMBER CUPS

    3 English (hothouse) cucumbers
    2 cups herbed cheese, such
       as Boursin
    ⅓ pound smoked salmon, cut
       in strips

Slice cucumbers into ½-inch rounds. Use hothouse cucumbers; they contain less moisture. Using a melon baller, remove the center of each round to make shallow cups. Fill with cheese and top with strip of salmon.

Makes 3 dozen appetizers.

CRAB TOASTS

    1 can (4 to 6 oz) crabmeat
    ¼ pound grated Cheddar cheese
    3 tablespoons mayonnaise
    ½ teaspoon Dijon mustard
       Dash hot-pepper sauce
    1 baguette

1. Drain crab. In a small bowl mix crab, Cheddar, mayonnaise, mustard, and hot-pepper sauce.

2. Slice baguette into ¼-inch rounds. Toast both sides. Spread mixture on toasts, broil until hot, then serve.

Makes 2 dozen rounds.

SMOKED CLAM LOG

    8 ounces cream cheese
    1½ tablespoons mayonnaise
    1 teaspoon Worcestershire sauce
       Dash hot-pepper sauce
    ⅛ teaspoon freshly ground
       white pepper
    1 can (4 oz) smoked clams,
       drained and chopped
       Chopped parsley (for garnish)

1. In a medium bowl combine cream cheese, mayonnaise, Worcestershire sauce, hot-pepper sauce, and pepper. Spread mixture on waxed paper to form a rectangle ¼ inch thick. Chill 1 hour.

2. Spread clams on cream cheese mixture and roll up like a jelly roll. Chill overnight. Before serving sprinkle parsley over roll and cut into ½-inch slices.

Makes about 2 dozen slices.

OYSTER-STUFFED CHERRY TOMATOES

    18 cherry tomatoes
    8 ounces cream cheese, at
       room temperature
    1 tablespoon chopped chives
    2 teaspoons Worcestershire sauce
       Dash hot-pepper sauce
    1 can (4 oz) smoked oysters,
       drained and chopped
       Chopped parsley (for garnish)

1. Cut thin slice from tops of tomatoes. Using melon baller carefully scoop out pulp, leaving shells intact.

2. In a medium bowl combine cream cheese, chives, Worcestershire sauce, hot-pepper sauce, and oysters. Fill each tomato cavity with oyster mixture and garnish with parsley.

Makes 18.

An age-old Japanese favorite, Sashimi, a dish made of raw fish that is served as a first course, has found new popularity in American cuisine.

UNCOOKED SEAFOOD

Among the many different ways to prepare fish, some age-old Japanese methods are extremely popular today. Sashimi and sushi are becoming increasingly available in restaurants and many sushi bars are opening across the country. These preparations require extremely fresh fish and shellfish. Never use a frozen fish; the fresh flavor critical to the dishes suffers.

Sashimi

Sashimi means raw fish cut into artful forms and served with different condiments that complement and provide a contrast to the mild flesh of the fish. Sashimi also refers to any shellfish served raw or on the half shell. Sashimi is part of any traditional meal in Japan and is always eaten first in order to savor the delicate flavors.

One of the most popular shapes is created by shaving paper-thin slices from the side of the fillet. This cut is appropriate for firm-fleshed fish such as sea bass or tuna. Lay the thin slices in an overlapping row to form a rosette, or wrap slices in toasted nori (dried sheets of seaweed), roll them like jelly rolls, and slice.

To toast nori, hold the rougher side of the sheet 2 to 3 inches from heating element until crispy, glossy, and slightly aromatic.

To serve sashimi, place an attractive arrangement of fish on the dish, and accompany with shredded daikon (a large white Japanese radish), shredded carrots and cucumbers, soy sauce, and wasabi paste (made from a green horseradishlike root with a hot taste).

Sushi

Sushi means vinegared rice garnished with an assortment of fish, shellfish, or vegetable pieces and served with various condiments. The history of sushi extends over a thousand years in Japan, where every area developed a sushi variation. Sushi may be rolled, wrapped, molded, or scattered.

To make good sushi it is important to cook the rice correctly. Proper preparation is not difficult, but it does require attention to detail to produce rice that remains tender and fluffy, not sticky. Use white short-grain Japanese rice. The shape of the sushi is determined by the different methods of molding rice.

The sushi most commonly seen in the United States is *nigiri-zushi* (*sushi* becomes *zushi* in a compound word), which consists of vinegared rice with toppings.

Other well-known sushis are *oshi-zushi* or pressed sushi (sushi rice and other ingredients pressed into a mold), *chirashi-zushi* (loosely packed sushi rice in bowls with topping scattered over top), and *maki-zushi* (rice and other ingredients rolled in sheets of toasted seaweed).

Sashimi is usually served on individual shallow dishes. Start with a very fresh fish fillet. Skin the fillet and trim off the thin sides to make it more rectangular. Remove bones with a pair of needlenose pliers or tweezers. The easiest shape to produce is a rectangle; slice fillet straight down and cut across the grain into strips. Another easy cut is the cube cut—simply cut fillet into ¾-inch dice.

SUSHI RICE

> 3⅓ cups short-grain rice, washed
> 4 cups water
> 5 tablespoons plus 1 teaspoon rice vinegar
> 5 tablespoons sugar
> 4 teaspoons salt

1. In a medium pot combine rice and water. Cover, bring water to a boil over high heat, and boil for 2 minutes. Reduce heat to medium and boil for 5 minutes.

2. Reduce heat to very low and cook for 15 minutes or until all water has been absorbed. (Do not check during the 15-minute cooking time or steam will escape.) Then remove pot from heat, take off lid, spread a clean kitchen towel over the top of the pot, replace the lid, and let stand for 10 to 15 minutes.

3. To prepare vinegar mixture, while rice is cooking, heat vinegar, sugar, and salt in a small pan over very low heat until sugar and salt dissolve. Place the pan in a bowl of ice to cool quickly, so the vinegar does not evaporate.

4. Empty cooked rice into a large, shallow wooden or plastic bowl or tray so rice can be spread in a thin layer. While spreading rice gently to prevent smashing the grains, sprinkle in vinegar mixture and toss to coat rice evenly. You may not need all of the vinegar mixture; do not add so much that the rice becomes mushy.

5. Ask another person to fan rice while you toss it, or blow air over rice with a small electric fan. Either procedure takes about 10 minutes to cool rice to room temperature.

6. To keep vinegared rice from drying after cooling, place rice in a container and cover with a damp cloth. Serve it the same day it is prepared. Do not refrigerate.

Makes 4 cups.

NIGIRI-ZUSHI

In Japanese culture, the balance of foods is very important, and it is considered bad form to disturb this balance. In sushi the balance is between the rice and accompanying ingredients. In nigiri-zushi there is more rice than topping—a good rule of thumb is to use twice as much rice as topping. Accompany with soy sauce, wasabi, and pickled ginger. Pickled ginger comes bottled in Oriental food shops. A variation of this recipe uses pickled garlic instead of the ginger. The garlic is also bottled and available at Oriental shops.

- 1 tablespoon rice vinegar
- ½ cup water
- 2 pounds raw fish
  Sushi Rice (see page 81)
- 2 tablespoons wasabi (Japanese horseradish)

1. Combine vinegar with water in a small bowl. This will be used to moisten hands while forming sushi.

2: Cut fish into rectangular finger-length slices about ⅛ inch thick, 1½ inches long, and ¾ inch wide. Moisten hands and pick up about 1½ tablespoons Sushi Rice. Shape into a roughly rectangular form about 1½ inches long and ¾ inch wide. Firmly but gently press and form rice on all sides.

3. Smear a dab of wasabi on a piece of fish, then press fish and rice together so that rice is roughly the length of the fish. Holding the sushi in one palm, use the other hand to press the edges of the rice to conform to the shape.

Makes 4 dozen pieces, about 8 servings.

OSHI-ZUSHI

This pressed sushi may be made in specialty molds found in Japanese markets or prepared in any mold that has a removable piece, such as a springform pan. Line the mold with something with a waxy finish, such as waxed paper. In Japan the leaves of the cast-iron plant, aspidistra, are often used. The object is to peel off the waxy layer after the sushi has been molded to preserve the shape of the sushi and prevent sticking.

- 1½ pounds fish or shellfish
- ½ cup rice vinegar
- ½ cup water
- 1 tablespoon rice vinegar
  Sushi Rice (see page 81)
  Wasabi to taste
- 2 sheets nori (seaweed), toasted

1. Cut fish into desired shape to fit mold, keeping thickness to about ¼ inch. Butterfly shrimp, if used. Place fish in the ½ cup vinegar and let sit for about 5 minutes.

2. Combine water and the 1 tablespoon vinegar. Use this mixture to moisten hands while forming sushi.

3. Line mold with waxed paper. Moisten hands with vinegar mixture and fill mold one-third full with rice. Pack down well. Remove fish from vinegar, pat dry, and layer in mold. Press down. Spread thin layer of wasabi on top. On top of fish, place a piece of nori cut to fit mold.

4. Add rice until mold is mounded with rice and press down firmly for about 30 seconds. Unmold sushi and slice with dampened knife.

Serves 6 to 8.

CHIRASHI-ZUSHI

The simplest type of sushi, the chirashi-zushi, is seafood and vegetables in or on vinegared rice. This sushi often includes cooked seafood, such as shrimp, and is sold as picnic food or box lunches in the railway stations of Japan. Dashi stock is sold in dried form in Japanese markets. It is a clear, fish-flavored soup stock used as a seasoning.

- 3 shiitake mushrooms
- ⅓ cup warm water
- ¼ cup dashi stock or Fish Fumet (see page 17)
- 2 tablespoons mirin
- 1½ tablespoons soy sauce
- 1 medium carrot, julienned
- ½ pound cooked bay shrimp
- ⅓ cup cooked green peas
  Sushi Rice (see page 81)

1. In a small bowl soak mushrooms in the warm water until soft, about 10 minutes. Remove, drain, and save water. Slice mushrooms into thin strips about ¼ inch wide, discarding the tough part of the stem.

2. In a small pan, add water saved from mushrooms to dashi or fumet, mirin, and soy sauce. Over medium heat blanch carrots until soft. Remove and drain. Cool sauce and add bay shrimp. Marinate for 15 minutes. Remove, drain, and discard liquid.

3. Reserve some mushroom strips, peas, carrots, and shrimp for garnish. In an attractive medium bowl, combine Sushi Rice, and remaining carrot, mushrooms, shrimp, and peas. Toss until well mixed. Garnish dish with reserved vegetables and shrimp.

Serves 6 to 8.

MAKI-ZUSHI

This rolled sushi is a great favorite as a takeout in Japan. You can make this sushi a few hours ahead of time, but the seaweed, nori, will not be as crisp. In an adaptation called California Roll, the ingredients are cooked crab, cooked shrimp, and fresh avocado. You need a mat to roll the sushi ingredients. Use an undyed, flexible straw place mat, or buy a special bamboo mat at an Asian market.

    4 sheets nori, toasted
       Sushi Rice (see page 81)
    1 cucumber
    1 pickled daikon (Japanese
       radish)
       Wasabi to taste
    ½ pound fish or shellfish,
       thinly sliced

1. Lay a sheet of nori on a bamboo mat. Spread one fourth of Sushi Rice on nori, leaving a 1-inch margin along the far edge of the nori and a ½-inch margin along either side. Flatten rice with back of a wooden spoon.

2. Cut strip of cucumber to equal the width of nori. Repeat with the pickled daikon. Place cucumber and daikon down center of nori (parallel to the long end). Spread with thin layer of wasabi. Place slice of fish down the center and gently press down to firm ingredients.

3. Lift bamboo mat with thumbs, holding ingredients with fingers, and roll so that the nori rolls around the filling. Roll tightly, and remove mat. Slice each roll into 6 to 8 pieces.

Makes 24 to 32 pieces.

Rolled and sliced, the multiple ingredients in Maki-Zushi form a beautiful mosaic. As an appetizer, Maki-Zushi adds Oriental elegance to almost any meal—formal or informal. Although made with fresh fish, the sushi can be prepared a few hours ahead and stored in the refrigerator.

GRAVLAX AND SEVICHE

Although it doesn't sound likely, fish may be cooked without heat. A marinade containing salt and acids (citrus juice or vinegar) breaks down connective tissues and firms up protein in much the same way heat does.

Marinated dishes include Scandinavian *gravlax* and Peruvian *seviche*. For gravlax, salmon is layered with a dry marinade of sugar, salt, herbs, and spices. Seviche employs the simplest form of pickling—marinating the food in an acid-based liquid.

GRAVLAX

Salt and sugar draw out juices, while the flavors of herbs and spices are absorbed by the fish.

- 1 *salmon (4 lbs), boned, head removed, skin intact*
- ¼ *cup kosher salt*
- ¼ *cup sugar*
- 1 *tablespoon crushed white peppercorns*
- 1 *cup chopped fresh dill*

Mustard Sauce

- 4 *tablespoons Creole mustard*
- 1 *teaspoon hot mustard, such as Colman's*
- 3 *tablespoons sugar*
- 2 *tablespoons white vinegar*
- ⅓ *cup vegetable oil*
- 2 *to 3 tablespoons chopped fresh dill*

1. Cut salmon into 2 pieces along the backbone. Wipe dry. Combine salt, sugar, and peppercorns, and rub fish on both sides with mixture. In a large, deep dish, sprinkle part of salt mixture, and one third of the dill. Lay one piece of fish in dish, sprinkle with one third of the dill, and some salt mixture. Lay other piece of fish on top of the first piece. Sprinkle with remaining salt and dill.

2. Cover tightly with foil, place heavy book or two bricks on top of foil to press down on fish. Refrigerate. After 4 to 6 hours some liquid will leach out; discard it. Refrigerate for 3 days, turning periodically so that the salt and seasonings penetrate evenly.

3. Before serving, drain fish on towel and scrape off the marinade. Place each fillet skin side down on serving board and cut thin diagonal slices across the grain. Serve with Mustard Sauce.

Serves 10 to 12.

Mustard Sauce In a small bowl combine all ingredients. Mix well.

SEVICHE

Putting limes in boiling water for 1 minute will yield more juice.

- 1½ *pounds white-fleshed fish*
- 1½ *cups lime juice*
- 1 *cup vegetable oil*
- 1 *cup orange juice*
- 1 *to 2 hot red chiles, seeded and slivered*
- 1 *small onion, sliced paper-thin*
- 1 *clove garlic, minced*
  Kosher salt and freshly ground pepper to taste

1. Remove skin and bones from the fish and cut into ½-inch cubes. Place fish in a small glass dish and cover with lime juice. It is extremely important that lime juice covers all of the fish. Add more if necessary.

2. Cover with plastic wrap and refrigerate for 4 to 5 hours. In the meantime, in a small bowl combine vegetable oil, orange juice, chiles, onion, and garlic. After fish has marinated for 3 hours, add this mixture and mix well. Chill for at least 2 more hours. Add salt and pepper to taste.

Serves 6 to 8.

SCALLOP SEVICHE

Any of the many small bay scallops may be used. If the scallops are small, they do not need to be sliced.

- 1 *pound sea scallops*
  Juice of 4 large limes
- 1 *teaspoon ground cumin*
  Half a medium white onion, sliced paper-thin
  Kosher salt and freshly ground pepper to taste
- ¼ *cup chopped fresh dill*

1. Cut scallops into small bite-sized pieces. Place in a small glass bowl. Cover scallops with lime juice and cumin.

2. Pour boiling water over onion slices, drain, and add onion to scallops along with salt, pepper, and dill. Make sure lime juice covers scallops. Refrigerate for at least 8 hours.

Serves 4 to 6.

TAHITIAN SEVICHE

Coconut milk lends a tropical touch to this warm weather seviche.

- 1 *pound fish*
- 2 *tablespoons kosher salt*
  Juice of 3 limes
- ⅓ *cup chopped green onion (include part of green)*
- ⅓ *cup coconut milk*

1. Cut fish into ½-inch cubes, removing skin and bones. Toss with salt. Let stand 2 to 3 hours until salt permeates fish. Rinse fish, leaving a trace of salt. Place fish in a small bowl and completely cover with lime juice, adding more if necessary.

2. Cover and refrigerate overnight. The next day, pour off juice. Cover fish with chopped onion and coconut milk. Serve very cold.

Serves 4.

CALIFORNIA SEVICHE

This colorful seviche makes a wonderful buffet centerpiece.

1½ pounds white-fleshed fish
   Juice of 6 large limes
3 medium tomatoes, peeled, seeded, and chopped
1 or 2 minced jalapeño or serrano chiles, chopped
⅓ cup olive oil
   Kosher salt and freshly ground pepper to taste
1 medium onion, sliced paper-thin
¼ cup chopped cilantro
2 large limes
3 avocados, peeled and sliced

1. Remove bones and skin from fish, and cut into ½-inch cubes. Place in a medium glass bowl. Cover fish with lime juice. Cover bowl and refrigerate until fish loses transparency and becomes opaque, at least 5 to 6 hours.

2. Drain juice from fish. Combine fish with tomato, chiles, olive oil, salt, pepper, onion, and cilantro. Squeeze juice from the 2 limes over mixture and toss well. Arrange sliced avocado on top, and serve.

Serves 6 to 8.

ESCABECHE

Escabeche is often served in the West Indies and in South America. The fish is partially cooked before being put into the marinade.

¼ cup peanut oil
2 cups thinly sliced onion
1 large clove garlic, minced
2 large eggs
1 tablespoon cold water
2 pounds fish, cut in 4-inch pieces
2 cups fine bread crumbs
1 large red bell pepper, seeded and sliced
1 whole clove, crushed
1 bay leaf, crushed
¼ cup very light red wine vinegar
½ cup water
   Kosher salt and freshly ground pepper to taste

1. In a large skillet heat oil. Add onion and garlic, and cook until soft—do not let ingredients brown. Remove from pan with slotted spoon, leaving oil in pan.

2. Beat eggs with the 1 tablespoon water. Pat fish dry with paper towels, then dip into beaten egg mixture. Dip into bread crumbs and sauté fish in oil used for onions and garlic. Cook about 1½ minutes on each side. Remove from heat and place fish in a large baking dish.

3. In a small saucepan place red pepper, clove, bay leaf, vinegar, the ½ cup water, salt, and pepper. Cook over medium heat for 3 minutes. Remove from heat and let cool. Pour over fish in baking dish and chill for several hours. Serve cold.

Serves 6 to 8.

Refreshingly light California Seviche is perfect for a summer entrée or as a first course. The cilantro and chile peppers enliven the taste, and the tomatoes and avocados brighten visual appeal.

ENTRÉES

The main course is most often the star of the meal, with all else taking second billing. When deciding on an entrée using fish or shellfish, you will find that the possibilities are almost limitless. A simple yet satisfying dish like Oysters and Eggs (recipe on page 100) could make a very special brunch. The elegant Fish in Puff Pastry (recipe on page 107) would be applauded by the most demanding palate. The soul-satisfying Fish and Seafood Jambalaya (recipe below) would please an entire crowd.

The following entrées can fit into any time schedule. Some must be prepared ahead, some can be quickly assembled and cooked with a flourish at the last minute.

FISH AND SEAFOOD JAMBALAYA

One of the top chefs in the country, Paul Prudhomme has always been in the vanguard when it comes to promoting American food and products. His Louisiana cuisine is like Chef Paul himself—honest and straightforward.

2 bay leaves
1½ teaspoons salt
1½ teaspoons ground red pepper
1½ teaspoons dried oregano
1¼ teaspoons white pepper
1 teaspoon black pepper
¾ teaspoon dried thyme
2½ tablespoons chicken fat, pork lard, beef fat, or butter
⅔ cup chopped tasso or other smoked ham (about 3 oz)
½ cup chopped andouille smoked sausage or smoked pork sausage such as kielbasa
1½ cups chopped onion
1 cup chopped celery
¾ cup chopped green bell pepper
1½ teaspoons minced garlic
4 cups peeled and chopped tomatoes (about 4 of medium size)
¾ cup tomato sauce
½ cup chopped green onion

2 cups uncooked rice, preferably converted
1 pound firm-fleshed fish fillets, cut in bite-sized pieces
18 oysters in their liquor (medium sized, about 10 oz)
18 medium shrimp (about ½ lb), peeled and deveined

Basic Seafood Stock

4 cups water
¾ to 1 pound rinsed shrimp heads and shells, crawfish heads and shells, crab shells, rinsed fish carcasses (heads and gills removed) in any combination (5 to 6 cups)
1 small onion, unpeeled and quartered
1 small rib celery
1 small clove garlic, unpeeled and quartered

1. Prepare Basic Seafood Stock. Preheat oven to 350° F.

2. Prepare seasoning mix in a small bowl by combining bay leaves, salt, red pepper, oregano, white pepper, black pepper, and thyme. Set aside.

3. In a 4-quart saucepan over medium heat, melt fat. Add ham and sausage; sauté until crisp (5 to 8 minutes), stirring frequently.

4. Add onion, celery, and pepper; sauté until tender but still firm (about 5 minutes), stirring occasionally and scraping pan bottom well.

5. Add seasoning mix and garlic; cook about 3 minutes, stirring constantly and scraping pan bottom as needed.

6. Add tomatoes and cook about 7 minutes, stirring frequently.

7. Add tomato sauce; cook about 7 minutes more, stirring fairly often.

8. Stir in stock and bring to a boil. Then stir in green onion and cook about 2 minutes, stirring once or twice.

9. Add rice, fish, oysters, and shrimp, stir well, and remove from heat.

10. Transfer mixture to an ungreased 9- by 13-inch baking pan. Cover pan snugly with aluminum foil and bake until rice is tender but still a bit crunchy (20 to 30 minutes). Remove from oven. If there is still liquid in the bottom of the pan, let pan sit a few minutes, still covered, to allow rice to absorb the liquid. Remove bay leaves.

11. To serve, mold jambalaya in an 8-ounce cup, and invert onto serving plates. Place 2 cups of jambalaya on each serving plate as a main course or 1 cup as an appetizer.

Serves 8 as an appetizer; serves 4 as a main dish.

Basic Seafood Stock Place water, seafood and shells, onion, celery, and garlic in a large saucepan; bring to a boil over high heat; reduce heat and simmer gently at least 4 hours, replenishing water as needed to keep about 2 cups of liquid in the pan. Strain, cool, and refrigerate until ready to use. (Note: If you are short on time, it is better to use a stock simmered 20 or 30 minutes than to use plain water. This is true for any recipe.)

Makes about 2 cups.

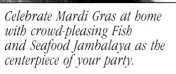

Celebrate Mardi Gras at home with crowd-pleasing Fish and Seafood Jambalaya as the centerpiece of your party.

Super Seafood Pizza is a new twist on an old favorite. Serve it either as a main dish or in bite-sized appetizer servings.

SUPER SEAFOOD PIZZA

Jane Helsel Joseph is a food professional whose extensive experience has come from work on the East and West coasts and in Europe. She created this pièce de résistance of pizzas.

    4 ounces shelled shrimp, cut
       in half lengthwise
    4 ounces (about 4 large)
       scallops, cut in quarters
 1½ tablespoons olive oil
    2 teaspoons lemon juice
    1 teaspoon minced peeled garlic
       Kosher salt and freshly
       ground pepper
  ⅓ cup peeled, thinly sliced
       red onion
  ½ cup sliced zucchini, cut
       in half-circles about
       ¼ inch thick
       Pizza dough for one
       12-inch pie
       Olive oil
    1 cup grated Gruyère or
       provolone cheese
  ⅓ cup seeded, diced tomato
       cut into ¾-inch pieces
       (one 3-oz tomato)
    3 tablespoons grated
       Parmesan cheese
    1 tablespoon chopped parsley

Rouille Sauce

    1 tablespoon dry white wine
       Pinch ground saffron
    1 tablespoon olive oil
  ⅛ to ¼ teaspoon crushed
       red pepper flakes
    1 large egg yolk
    1 teaspoon fresh lemon juice
  ½ teaspoon minced peeled garlic
  ⅛ teaspoon kosher salt
  ¼ cup olive oil
    1 tablespoon chopped fresh basil

1. In a small bowl toss shrimp, scallops, 1 tablespoon of the olive oil, lemon juice, ½ teaspoon of the garlic, and a sprinkling of salt and pepper. Marinate 30 to 45 minutes. Drain through a sieve, and discard marinade. Preheat oven to 425° F.

2. Heat the remaining ½ tablespoon olive oil in a small to medium skillet. Add remaining ½ teaspoon garlic and onion. Stirring constantly, cook about 20 seconds over high heat. Add the zucchini and cook, stirring constantly, another 20 seconds. Remove from heat and set aside.

3. Oil pizza pan; set aside. Form dough to fit pan. Brush entire surface with olive oil. Sprinkle ½ cup of the Gruyère over the top of the dough, leaving a 1-inch border. Strew the cooked onion, garlic, and zucchini over the cheese; top with tomato. Sprinkle remaining ½ cup Gruyère over the top. Sprinkle with salt and pepper.

4. Bake until almost done and crust is nicely browned, 15 to 20 minutes. Remove the pizza from the oven. Preheat broiler. Adjust the upper rack if necessary. Scatter the scallops and shrimp over the pizza. Place under broiler until seafood is almost done, 1 to 2 minutes. Remove again and spoon Rouille Sauce over top. Sprinkle with Parmesan and pepper. Return pizza to broiler until the sauce is bubbly, about 2 minutes. Remove from the oven, and sprinkle with parsley. Let rest 5 minutes before serving.

Makes 8 slices.

Rouille Sauce Don't be tempted to use a food processor or electric blender; the consistency will not be the same. Mix wine and saffron in a small dish. Set near the stove and steep for at least 10 minutes. Heat oil in a small skillet. Add pepper and cook 10 seconds. Remove skillet from heat and add wine-saffron mixture. Stand back—it will sizzle. Let cool. In a small mixing bowl, whisk egg yolk with lemon juice, garlic, and salt. Gradually begin adding oil, drop by drop, whisking continuously. As sauce begins to thicken, add oil a little faster. When all oil is added, stir in pepper mixture and basil.

Makes about ⅓ cup.

LARDED SEA BASS FILLET WITH SOUR CREAM AND CABBAGE

Ken Wolfe is a professional chef and instructor who has been responsible for training many a fine chef. He created this unusual, exceptionally tasty dish. Serve with new boiled potatoes.

  36 lardons, cut from about 8
       ounces slab bacon, half
       frozen (see step 1 below)
    6 sea bass fillets (6 oz each)
    4 tablespoons unsalted butter
  12 cups cubed cabbage
    1 to 2 tablespoons sugar
    1 teaspoon dried thyme
       Salt and white pepper to taste
    2 cups sour cream
    2 tablespoons flour
    1 tablespoon imported paprika
  ½ cup or more dry white wine
       Lemon wedges (for garnish)
       Parsley sprigs (for garnish)

1. To prepare lardons, cut "matchsticks" of half-frozen bacon, each measuring about ⅜ by ⅜ by 1¾ inches.

2. Lard each portion of fish with 6 lardons, distributed evenly. (With tip of a sharp knife, make 6 small slits in fish, and insert lardons with finger.) Place larded side up in a large, buttered roasting dish or pan.

3. In a large sauté pan, melt butter. Sauté cabbage until al dente, or still slightly crisp. Add sugar, thyme, salt, and pepper. Keep warm.

4. In a medium pan combine sour cream, flour, paprika, and wine. Bring to a boil, stirring, and cook until you have a light sauce. To thin sauce, add wine; to thicken, reduce it.

5. Preheat broiler. Place fish under broiler until bacon ends are brown. If fish is browned but not done, turn broiler off, and bake fish at 425° F until done. Place cabbage on plate, top with fish, and nap (half cover) with the sauce. Garnish with lemon wedges and parsley.

Serves 6.

SCALLOP-AND-CRAB MOUSSE WITH SPINACH AND YELLOW PEPPER SAUCE

Amey Shaw is a classically trained chef who has worked in Bay Area restaurants for the past seven years. Now executive chef at the Fourth Street Grill in Berkeley, California, she created this beautiful dish while chef of the Pavilion Room at Oakland's Claremont Resort Hotel.

    1 pound bay scallops
    2 to 3 egg whites
    2 teaspoons salt
    ½ teaspoon white pepper
    ½ teaspoon cayenne pepper
    ¼ teaspoon ground nutmeg
    1 cup whipping cream
    6 ounces crabmeat
    1 pound spinach
    1 red bell pepper
    2 tablespoons clarified
       butter (see page 114)

Yellow Pepper Sauce

    6 yellow bell peppers
    1 cup whipping cream
    ⅓ to ½ cup Roux (see page 114)
    4 tablespoons clarified butter
       (see page 114)
    6 shallots, finely minced
    1 clove garlic, finely minced
    ½ cup Fish Fumet
       (see page 17)

1. Preheat oven to 350° F. Place scallops, egg whites, salt, white pepper, cayenne, and nutmeg in a food processor fitted with steel blade. Process until smooth. With machine running, very slowly add the cream. Strain purée through sieve into a medium stainless steel bowl set over ice.

2. Add crab and gently blend with a rubber spatula. Test for taste and consistency. The mousse should resemble a thick paste. Put a test amount in a buttered ramekin

and steam for 5 minutes, or bake in a water bath in the oven for 20 minutes. If the mousse is too thick, add more cream. If not thick enough, add more egg white.

3. Butter six 3-ounce ramekins and pack them with the mousse. Place a towel on the work surface and firmly bang each ramekin to force air out. Butter 6 rounds of parchment or wax paper and cover each ramekin, buttered side down. Set ramekins in large pan. Place in preheated oven.

4. Carefully pour boiling water into pan, making sure you do not splash into mousse. Water should reach halfway up the sides of the ramekins. Bake approximately 20 minutes. Before removing, test as you would a cake; mousse is done when a toothpick inserted in the middle of the mousse comes out clean. Prepare sauce while mousse bakes.

5. Throughly clean spinach, remove stems, and dry. Remove stems, seeds, and veins from red bell pepper and finely chop. Heat a large skillet and melt clarified butter. Add spinach and toss until spinach is slightly wilted, about 30 seconds.

6. Arrange spinach on plates and unmold mousse on top. Pour Yellow Pepper Sauce over top and garnish with a sprinkling of chopped red pepper.

Serves 6 as an appetizer or first course.

Yellow Pepper Sauce

1. Wash peppers. Remove stems, seeds, and veins and chop coarsely. In a medium pot with a heavy bottom, heat cream. After it comes to a boil, add enough roux to thicken slightly. Simmer 30 minutes.

2. In a medium pan melt butter and cook shallots gently until translucent but not brown. Add peppers. Stir until evenly coated, then add garlic and fumet. Simmer until soft, about 10 minutes. Remove from heat and cool slightly.

3. Purée in processor until smooth, then strain. Strain the cream mixture through a sieve into the pepper mixture. Taste for seasoning. The sauce must be tasty but should not overwhelm the mousse.

SEA BASS IN ALMOND SAUCE
Rebalo almendrado

Marge Poore is a cooking instructor specializing in Mexican and Latin American foods. Her yearly tours to Mexico help her develop great new recipes. The flavors in this dish are classic in Mexican cuisine.

    1½ pounds sea bass fillets
        Salt and pepper
    4   tablespoons unsalted butter
    2   to 3 cloves garlic,
        finely chopped
    6   green onions, sliced in
        rounds (use part of green)
    ¾   cup finely chopped
        almonds, toasted in the skin
    1   or 2 serrano chiles,
        finely chopped
    ¼   cup lime juice
    ½   to ¾ cup chopped cilantro,
        loosely packed

1. Preheat oven to 350° F. Place fillets in a medium buttered baking dish. Sprinkle lightly with salt and pepper. Set aside.

2. In small skillet melt butter over medium heat. Add garlic and onion. Sauté for about 1 minute. Stir in almonds, chiles, lime juice, and salt and pepper to taste. Distribute mixture over fish. Sprinkle on cilantro.

3. Cover with foil and bake for about 10 to 20 minutes, depending on the thickness of fish. Serve with sauce spooned over each portion.

Serves 6.

SEAFOOD BASTILLA

Loni Kuhn's great zest for life is reflected in her country and ethnic foods with robust flavors. A beloved member of the food world, she shares this seafood recipe.

- ½ cup unsalted butter
- ½ pound mushrooms, thinly sliced
- 3 cloves garlic, minced
- 1 tablespoon sweet imported paprika
- Salt and freshly ground pepper
- 1 teaspoon cayenne pepper
- ½ teaspoon ground cumin
- ½ to 1 teaspoon packed saffron threads
- ½ teaspoon turmeric
- 2 tablespoons flour
- 1 cup or more Fish Fumet (page 17)
- ½ cup chopped parsley
- ½ cup chopped cilantro
- 7 large eggs, lightly beaten
- 1 pound red snapper, cut in 1-inch pieces
- ⅓ pound crabmeat, cooked
- ⅓ pound bay shrimp, cooked
- 1 pound filo dough (about 27 sheets)
- Melted butter to brush filo

1. Melt butter in large sauté pan and add mushrooms, garlic, paprika, salt, pepper, cayenne, cumin, saffron, and turmeric. Sauté a few minutes. Add flour and cook 2 minutes more. Add fumet, stir, and simmer for 2 minutes. Add parsley, cilantro, and eggs. Cook, stirring and scraping the bottom of the pan until soft curds form. Add fish and cook 2 minutes. Add crab and shrimp and immediately remove from pan to a large bowl. The mixture may be set aside for several hours until you are ready to fill the filo.

2. Place 7 or 8 sheets of filo in a 12-inch pizza pan, arranging them so they fan out from the center and overlap, resembling the petals of a flower. Filo sheets should extend beyond the edge of the pan. Lightly brush each sheet with butter. Place 4 or 5 more sheets, each buttered and folded in half, in the center of the pan to reinforce the bottom. Spread filling in pan. Brush the exposed edges of filo with more butter. Fold filo back over the filling. Lay 7 or 8 more sheets on top, brushing each with butter. Invert onto another pizza pan, and lay 5 or 6 more sheets on this new top, brushing with butter as before. Tuck in the edges neatly, trimming if necessary. At this point the assembled bastilla can be set aside for up to 3 hours before baking.

3. Preheat oven to 350° F. Bake until risen, crisp, and golden brown, about 30 minutes. It is desirable to invert the bastilla halfway through baking to enhance crispness.

Serves 8.

Bastilla is the Middle-Eastern counterpart to American one-dish meals. The crisp filo dough can hold a variety of different fillings such as poultry or lamb mixtures. This version includes a savory blend of fish and shellfish richly flavored with exotic spices.

Lemon Pasta

1¾ cups flour
2 large eggs
¼ cup lemon juice
   Zest of 1 lemon
½ teaspoon salt
2 tablespoons flour

1. Prepare Lemon Pasta and set aside.

2. In medium pan heat cream and reduce until 1½ cups remain. Add ¼ cup of the Parmesan cheese, green onion, artichoke hearts, and crab-meat, and cook over low heat until just heated through.

3. Meanwhile bring salted water to a boil. Add the Lemon Pasta and cook until al dente (firm to the bite), about 1 minute. Drain and toss with the butter.

4. Pour the sauce over the pasta and toss. Sprinkle the remaining Parmesan on top. Season with salt and pepper. Serve immediately.

Serves 4 as a main course; serves 6 as an appetizer.

Lemon Pasta Place flour on work surface and make a well in the center. Break eggs into the well, add lemon juice, lemon zest, and salt; mix with fork. Gradually add flour to liquid until a ball of dough forms. Knead dough for 8 minutes or until it forms a smooth, elastic ball. Wrap dough in waxed paper and let rest at least 30 minutes. Following manufacturer's instructions for your pasta machine, roll out dough one third at a time and cut into thin noodles. Toss formed pasta with 2 tablespoons flour to prevent pasta from sticking.

Crab and Artichoke Hearts With Lemon Pasta is a rich, delicious dish and is deceptively easy to prepare. Pasta is made with a simple dough that is fed through a pasta machine—that's all there is to it. The taste of home-made pasta is far superior to that of most commercially prepared products, and you can add any flavorings you like.

CRAB AND ARTICHOKE HEARTS WITH LEMON PASTA

Diane Gould created this recipe. The fresh lemon pasta is a wonderful contrast to the richness of the crab and artichoke hearts.

3 cups whipping cream
½ cup freshly grated
   Parmesan cheese
½ cup thinly sliced green
   onion (use part of green)
1 jar (4½ oz) artichoke
   hearts, drained, rinsed, and
   coarsely chopped
2 cups crabmeat
8 quarts salted water
¼ cup unsalted
   butter, at room temperature
   Salt and freshly
   ground pepper

CROUSTADE OF SEA SCALLOPS

Gerard N. Collet, an instructor at the California Culinary Academy, created this French classic.

    4 thick (¾ in.) slices
       white bread
    1 cup clarified butter (see
       page 114)
    1 pound fresh scallops
       Salt and freshly ground
       white pepper
    ¼ cup milk or beer
    1 tablespoon flour
    3 cloves garlic, minced
    3 shallots, minced
       Lemon slices and parsley
       sprigs (for garnish)

Tomato Concassée

    2 large tomatoes
    1 tablespoon olive oil
       Herbes de Provence to taste

1. *To prepare croustades:* Trim crusts from each slice of bread. Then carve out an inside rectangle ¼ inch from each side and ¼ inch from the bottom. (To make bottom cut, make a slit in the end of the bread and insert knife.) Remove inside rectangle. In medium sauté pan heat ¼ cup of the clarified butter and lightly brown croustades. Keep croustades warm. Prepare Tomato Concassée.

2. *To prepare scallops:* Sprinkle scallops with salt and pepper. Dip scallops in milk or beer, then into flour. Pat dry to remove excess flour. In medium sauté pan heat remaining ¾ cup clarified butter. Add scallops, shallots, and garlic. Cook until scallops are golden.

3. *To assemble the dish:* Place scallops in croustades and garnish with Tomato Concassée, lemon slices, and parsley.

Serves 4.

Tomato Concassée Peel, seed, and roughly chop tomatoes. In small sauté pan heat oil and add tomatoes and Herbes de Provence. Cook until tomatoes dry out slightly.

COULIBIAC

Susan Walter is a talented cook. Busy as a caterer and cooking instructor, she is also president of the San Francisco Professional Food Society. Her recipe is a wonderful and elegant creation.

Brioche

    1   tablespoon active dry yeast
    1   teaspoon sugar
    ¼   cup warm water
    3   eggs
    2¼ cups flour
    1   teaspoon salt
    10 tablespoons unsalted butter

Sole Mousse

    2   pounds sole fillets, cut
        in pieces
    2   egg whites
        Salt
        Freshly ground white pepper
        Freshly grated nutmeg
    1½ to 2 cups whipping cream

Duxelles

    2   tablespoons unsalted butter
    3   shallots, minced
    ½   pound mushrooms, finely
        chopped
    3   tablespoons dry white wine
        Salt and freshly
        ground pepper
    2   tablespoons whipping cream

For Assembly

    2   eggs, beaten with 1
        tablespoon water
    1   salmon fillet, 1 inch
        thick (8 oz)
    12 to 15 large spinach leaves

1. *To make brioche:* In large bowl of electric mixer, dissolve yeast and sugar in the warm water. Beat in eggs, flour, and salt. Beat 1 minute. Cover and let rise 1 hour. Beat in butter and let rise 1 more hour.

2. *To prepare sole mousse:* Make certain the fish, egg whites, and cream are cold; this allows the mousse to absorb more cream. In food processor fitted with steel blade, place the sole, egg whites, salt, pepper, and nutmeg. Purée, then, with machine running, slowly add 1½ to 2 cups cream, depending on desired texture. When cream has been absorbed, stop machine and chill mousse until needed.

3. *To prepare duxelles:* In a medium sauté pan, melt butter. Add shallots and sauté 1 minute. Add mushrooms, wine, salt, and pepper. Cook over low heat until all the moisture has evaporated from the mushrooms, about 20 minutes. When the mixture begins to look dry, add the cream and continue to cook until mixture is quite thick. Remove from heat and reserve.

4. *To assemble the dish:* Preheat oven to 350° F. Roll out brioche dough in a rectangle about ½ inch thick, 10 inches wide by 20 inches long. Brush dough with the 2 eggs beaten with water. Spread duxelles over dough to within 2 inches of sides and 5 inches of ends. Spread half of the sole mousse over duxelles. Wrap salmon in spinach leaves and place in center of sole mousse. Cover with remaining mousse. Wrap dough around filling, sealing edges with water. Bake for 50 minutes.

Serves 8 as a first course.

FISH CASSEROLE WITH PARSLEY SAUCE

The Charlotte Combe Cooking School is a highly respected cooking school in Redwood City, California. Charlotte Combe, versed in classical French techniques and a protégée of Jacques Pepin, offers this classic recipe from her Scottish homeland.

- 2½ *pounds potatoes, washed and peeled*
- 6 *to 8 tablespoons unsalted butter*
- ¼ *cup milk*
  Dash freshly ground white pepper
  Dash freshly grated nutmeg
- ½ *cup finely chopped green onion*
- ¼ *cup finely chopped parsley*
- 8 *fillets of sole (4 to 6 oz each)*
  Salt and pepper
- ½ *cup dry white wine*
- ¼ *cup water*
- ½ *teaspoon fresh thyme*
- 8 *ounces shrimp meat (optional)*

Parsley Sauce

- ¼ *cup unsalted butter*
- 3 *tablespoons flour*
- 2½ *to 3 cups milk*
- ¼ *teaspoon salt*
  Dash ground nutmeg
  Dash freshly ground white pepper
- ¾ *cup finely chopped parsley*

1. Cook potatoes in boiling salted water until tender. Drain and pass through a food mill. Stir in butter, milk, white pepper, and nutmeg. Set aside.

2. Preheat oven to 350° F. In a small bowl, mix green onion and parsley. Trim and remove bones from sole. Sprinkle with salt, pepper, and onion mixture. Fold each fillet in half and place in medium ovenproof dish.

Add wine, water, and thyme. Cover with parchment paper and cook about 20 minutes. Cooking time depends on the thickness of fillets. Do not overcook the fish. Prepare Parsley Sauce while fish cooks.

3. Increase oven temperature to 375° F. Using a spatula, transfer fillets to an ovenproof serving dish, arranging them so that a 2-inch border remains all around. Sprinkle the shrimp meat (if used) between the fillets. Pour Parsley Sauce over fish. Then, using a pastry bag fitted with a large open-star tip, pipe the potatoes around the edge of the dish. Bake until piping hot. The casserole may be placed under a broiler for a few seconds to brown the potatoes.

Serves 8.

Parsley Sauce In a medium saucepan melt butter, then stir in flour, whisking over medium heat for a few seconds. Stir in milk and simmer gently for 10 minutes. Add salt, nutmeg, pepper, and parsley. A little of the poaching liquid may be added to this sauce to impart extra flavor.

ENGLISH DRESSED FISH

Tina Salter trained at the London Cordon Bleu. While she was living in London and working as a caterer, her specialty became dressed salmon. Though a bit time-consuming, it is certainly a spectacular dish.

- 1 *salmon (7 to 9 lbs), cleaned and scaled*
  Wine Court Bouillon (see page 16)
- 3 *tablespoons lemon juice*
- 3 *tablespoons water*
- 1 *envelope (1 tablespoon) unflavored gelatin*
- 6 *cups Aspic (see page 122)*
- 2 *cups Basic Mayonnaise (see page 117)*
  Garnish of watercress, sliced cucumber, pimiento, chives, and sliced carrot in any combination

1. Prepare salmon by washing well. Place whole fish into warm court bouillon, bring to simmer, and poach until done. Check for doneness by pulling back a fin—it should come away clean, but the flesh should still be firm. Allow fish to cool in court bouillon. You may add ice to speed cooling.

2. Mix lemon juice and water, and dissolve gelatin in this mixture. Add 1½ cups of the aspic to the mayonnaise and stir gently to mix well, without incorporating air into the mixture. Stir dissolved gelatin into mayonnaise mixture.

3. Place cool salmon on a rack above a tray. With a sharp knife score skin around head and tail. The skin at the ends remains. The skin between the two cuts is to be removed completely; take care not to scrape the flesh. Remove back fin and any bones that protrude from the head.

4. Coat exposed flesh of salmon with mayonnaise mixture. Place in refrigerator until set. Repeat the coating process a second time to give a smooth covering. Again place in refrigerator until set. Prepare garnish of watercress, cucumbers, pimiento, chives, and carrots. Dip each decoration in aspic before placing it on fish. The aspic will set and adhere the decoration to the salmon. Allow to set again.

5. Coat decorated fish with clear aspic mixture; two or three coats may be necessary to give a complete covering and a deep shine. Allow aspic to set each time in refrigerator. When set, remove from tray and place on serving dish. Decorate dish with thinly sliced cucumbers. Lightly coat cucumbers with aspic and chill. Serve chilled.

Serves 12 to 24.

Chaud-froid is a classic preparation in which a cooked, chilled food, such as this trout, is coated with sauce and glazed with aspic.

Four-Onion Soufflé is creamier than traditional recipes. Far from overpowering the flavor of the shrimp it contains, the four members of the onion family combine to give this dish a subtly different taste. Served as an entrée, luncheon dish, or first-course specialty, it is attractive and elegant, yet easy to prepare.

PAN-FRIED PERCH WITH PECANS

Bradley Ogden is one of the Young Turks in American cooking. This talented young chef's menus reflect the vast bounty and tradition of this country and show great pride in our food heritage. Note that the perch soaks in milk overnight.

    12 perch (6 oz each)
     4 cups milk
     3 tablespoons kosher salt
     2 tablespoons ground white
         pepper
     1 teaspoon hot-pepper sauce
    1½ cups clarified butter (see
         page 114)

     1 cup unsalted butter
     2 cups chopped pecans
         Juice of 3 lemons
     1 cup chopped parsley
     2 tablespoons kosher salt
     1 teaspoon freshly ground
         pepper

Pecan Flour

     2 cups pecan pieces
    1½ cups yellow cornmeal
     ½ cup flour
     2 tablespoons kosher salt
     1 teaspoon freshly ground
         black pepper

1. Clean perch. In a large bowl combine milk, the 3 tablespoons salt, white pepper, and hot-pepper sauce. Soak fish overnight in seasoned milk.

2. Divide clarified butter and place into two large skillets. Heat until very hot, then reduce heat to medium. Remove the perch from the milk and dredge in Pecan Flour, coating evenly. Place in skillets and cook until golden brown on both sides. Remove from skillets and set aside.

3. Remove excess grease from one skillet. Add the 1 cup butter and pecans and brown. Remove from heat and add lemon juice, parsley, salt, and pepper. Serve two perch per plate with a spoonful of pecan-butter mixture over fish.

Serves 6.

Pecan Flour Use food processor to grind pecans finely. In a medium bowl, combine ground pecans, cornmeal, flour, salt, and pepper. Mix well.

FOUR-ONION SOUFFLÉ

This soufflé has a heavier texture than a traditional soufflé. It unmolds beautifully, showing a crusty brown exterior and creamy oniony interior. It is even good cold the next day. Serve with a crisp green salad.

> 1 *cup dry bread crumbs*
> 5 *tablespoons unsalted butter*
> ¾ *cup finely minced yellow onion*
> ¼ *cup minced green onion*
> ¼ *cup minced shallot*
> 5 *tablespoons flour*
> 1 *cup Lemon Crème Fraîche (see page 119)*
> 1 *teaspoon salt*
> ¼ *teaspoon white pepper*
> ¼ *cup chopped chives*
> 1 *pound bay shrimp, chopped*
> 8 *egg whites*

1. Preheat oven to 375° F. Heavily butter a 1½-quart soufflé dish, then add bread crumbs. Rotate dish until crumbs line sides and bottom, then shake out any excess. Set dish

aside. In small sauté pan, melt 2 tablespoons of the butter. Add onion, green onion, and shallot. Sauté until onions are soft and moisture has evaporated. Set aside.

2. In small saucepan, make a roux by melting remaining 3 tablespoons butter, adding flour, and cooking over medium heat while whisking constantly. Remove from heat, add crème fraîche, and continue to whisk rapidly. Return to low heat, whisking until thick. Remove from heat and add salt, pepper, chives, cooked onions, and shrimp.

3. Beat egg whites to soft-peak stage. Take a heaping tablespoon of egg whites and mix into onion mixture. Working quickly and carefully, fold in the rest of the onion mixture. Fill prepared soufflé dish with mixture. Bake until toothpick inserted in center comes out clean, 30 to 40 minutes. Let rest for 2 to 3 minutes, then unmold on serving plate.

Serves 6.

BRAISED TROUT WITH AROMATIC SAUCE

Rose Hansen is a West Coast food writer who develops and tests recipes and styles food for photographs. This recipe shows her great style in taste, presentation, and ease of preparation.

> 2 *tablespoons vegetable oil*
> 2 *tablespoons unsalted butter*
> 1 *medium carrot, peeled and chopped*
> *Half a medium onion, peeled and chopped*
> 1 *rib celery, trimmed and chopped*
> 1 *clove garlic, peeled and minced*
> 4 *whole trout (about 1 lb each), cleaned, head and tail left attached*
> *Salt and freshly ground pepper to taste*
> ½ *cup dry vermouth*
> 1 *tablespoon chopped fresh basil, or 1½ teaspoons dried*
> 1 *teaspoon fresh thyme or ½ teaspoon dried*
> 2 *tablespoons unsalted butter, cut in pieces*
> *Minced parsley (for garnish)*

1. Heat oil and 2 tablespoons butter in large skillet; sauté carrot, onion, celery, and garlic over low heat until vegetables are soft, about 10 minutes.

2. Lightly season trout with salt and pepper. Add trout, vermouth, basil, and thyme to skillet. Cook, covered, until fish flakes easily with fork, 5 to 8 minutes. Transfer fish to a warm serving platter. Strain vegetables and surround trout with them. Keep warm.

3. Reduce cooking liquid to ¼ cup over high heat; whisk in 2 tablespoons butter, bit by bit, until sauce is smooth and slightly thickened. Pour over fish. Garnish with parsley.

Serves 4.

BURRIDA

Ric O'Connell is one of the first ladies of food in San Francisco and is well known for her culinary expertise. Her creations, like this talented woman, are always exciting.

    3½ to 4 pounds assorted fish
    ¾   cup olive oil
    2   large cloves garlic
    1   medium onion, chopped
    2   anchovy fillets, minced
    ¼   cup parsley, chopped
    1   cup crushed tomatoes
    10 walnuts, pounded or
        processed
    1¼ cups white wine
    1   bay leaf
        Freshly ground pepper
        French bread
        Olive oil, 1 inch deep, for
        frying

1. Cut fish into serving-sized pieces. In a large sauté pan heat the ¾ cup olive oil and sauté garlic. Press garlic into oil, then discard cloves.

2. In same oil sauté onion until soft. Add anchovy, parsley, tomatoes, walnuts, and wine. Over high heat boil liquid until it is reduced by about one fourth.

3. Add fish and bay leaf. Sprinkle with pepper to taste. Simmer until fish is done, 10 to 20 minutes; cooking time depends on size of fish.

4. Meanwhile cut bread into ¼-inch slices. Heat 1 inch olive oil in a medium skillet and sauté bread on both sides to toast. Serve fish over toast.

Serves 8.

CRAYFISH PIE

M. Susan Broussard studied at Le Cordon Bleu and La Varenne in Paris. By combining her cooking skills with creativity, she has become an expert at styling food for photographic sessions. She adapted this from her mother's crayfish *étouffée* recipe. Crayfish fat is available frozen from fish markets.

    1   pound steamed crayfish
        tails, peeled
        Cayenne pepper, black pepper,
        and salt to taste
    3   onions, finely chopped
    ¼   cup peanut oil
    ¼   teaspoon garlic, pressed
    1   tablespoon finely chopped
        green bell pepper
    1   cup butter
    2   to 3 tablespoons crayfish fat
    1   tablespoon paprika
    ½   cup water
    1   tablespoon cornstarch
    ¼   cup finely chopped green
        onion
    1   tablespoon finely chopped
        parsley
        Hot-pepper sauce to taste

Pastry

    3   cups flour, sifted
    ⅔   cup unsalted butter, softened
    2   egg yolks, at room
        temperature
    1   teaspoon salt
    6   to 10 tablespoons ice water

1. Prepare Pastry. In a medium bowl season crayfish with cayenne, black pepper, and salt. Toss and set aside. In a large, heavy pan, sauté onion in peanut oil without browning. Add garlic and green pepper; sauté lightly. Add butter and crayfish fat, reduce heat, and cook until oil rises. Add seasoned crayfish and paprika, stirring well. Add ¼ cup of the water, increase temperature, and heat through.

2. Mix cornstarch with about 2 tablespoons of remaining water. When the crayfish gravy begins to bubble around the sides of the pan, add as much cornstarch mixture as is necessary to give body to the gravy. Stir well, add green onion, parsley, and hot-pepper sauce. Correct seasonings. Do not overcook crayfish or they will become tough.

3. Divide Pastry in two pieces, one slightly larger than the other. Roll larger piece out to fit a 9- or 10-inch pie pan and use it to line the pan. Pour crayfish mixture into pie shell. Roll remaining pastry to fit over pie, and place it on the pie. Refrigerating or freezing the unbaked pie enhances flavor. To store, wrap tightly in plastic. Refrigerate for at least 30 minutes and as long as 2 days. Defrost the pie before baking.

4. To bake, preheat oven to 350° F. Bake pie for 15 minutes, then lower temperature to 300° F until golden brown, about 12 minutes.

Serves 8.

Pastry Place flour on a marble board or flat surface. Make a well in flour and place butter, yolks, salt, and 4 tablespoons ice water in the well. Work butter, salt, and yolks together with fingertips of one hand. Gradually work in flour by cutting mixture with a pastry scraper. (This indispensable tool makes all of the difference in preparing pie crust. It resembles a spatula without a handle.) Add water a tablespoon at a time if crumbs are dry. When pastry resembles large peas, push dough away with the heel of one hand until all of the dough has been smeared across the board. Gather dough up using the scraper. Press dough into a ball and refrigerate until ready to roll out.

Makes 1 double-crust 9- to 10-inch pie shell.

RISOTTO WITH SMOKED SALMON

A favorite at the Villa d'Este in Italy, this risotto should be made with arborio, an Italian rice. Cooked as specified, the rice remains *al dente*—firm and chewy. For variations, use cooked clams or mussels instead of salmon. Or substitute ½ pound cleaned, sliced squid sautéed in 3 tablespoons of butter.

- 6 *tablespoons unsalted butter*
- ¼ *cup minced onion*
- 2 *cups arborio rice*
- 3 *to 5 cups Fish Fumet (page 17), heated*
- ⅔ *cup slivered smoked salmon*
- 3 *tablespoons unsalted butter*
- 4 *tablespoons freshly grated Parmesan cheese*
  Freshly ground white pepper
- 3 *tablespoons chopped parsley*

1. In a large, heavy pan, melt the 6 tablespoons butter, add onion, and cook slowly until onion is soft. Add rice to pan, stirring until grains of rice are coated completely.

2. In a small sauce pan, heat the Fish Fumet. When it is hot, add 1 cup of the fumet to the butter and rice mixture and stir constantly until liquid is absorbed. Add fumet ½ cup at a time, stirring continuously and allowing rice to absorb liquid before adding more. Test rice as it cooks. When cooked, the mixture is creamy, but each grain of rice retains its shape and is al dente in the center.

3. Add salmon and the 3 tablespoons butter. Stir well, sprinkle with Parmesan, pepper, and parsley. Serve as soon as possible.

Serves 8.

More and more people are discovering the delicate taste of crayfish. If you've never before tasted this freshwater shellfish, Crayfish Pie is a great way to start. It is a rich and satisfying dish for an informal brunch or supper.

SALADE DE SAINT-JACQUES
Scallop salad

Elizabeth Thomas, trained at the London Cordon Bleu, has had a cooking school in the hills of Berkeley, California, since 1977.

- 1 pound sea scallops
- 2 cups chicken stock
- 48 small, fresh asparagus spears, 3 inches long
- 1 package enoki mushrooms
- 1 egg
- 2 egg yolks
- 1 tablespoon Dijon mustard
- ¾ teaspoon salt
  Freshly ground white pepper
- 1 tablespoon white wine vinegar
- 2 tablespoons lemon juice
  Pinch cayenne pepper
- 1½ cups vegetable oil
- 2 tablespoons tomato paste
- 1 tablespoon prepared horseradish
- 3 tablespoons gin
- ½ cup whipping cream
- 1 bunch watercress, stemmed

1. *To prepare salad:* Rinse and clean scallops. In a medium pan bring stock to a boil, then add scallops. Remove immediately from heat, cover, and let stand 5 minutes. Remove lid and let cool.

2. Cook asparagus in boiling salted water until crisp-tender. Drain, plunge into cold water, and drain again. Trim roots from mushrooms.

3. *To prepare sauce:* Process egg, egg yolks, mustard, salt, pepper, vinegar, lemon juice, cayenne, and ¼ cup of the vegetable oil in food processor for 5 seconds. With machine running, slowly pour in remaining 1¼ cups vegetable oil. Add tomato paste, horseradish, gin, and cream; process briefly. Chill.

4. *To assemble:* Spread ¼ cup sauce over each of 8 plates. Arrange sliced scallops in an overlapping circle around a small bunch of watercress in the center of each plate. Alternate asparagus and mushrooms like spokes of a wheel around scallops.

Serves 8.

GUMBO CORDON ROUGE

Jay Perkins, the creator of this recipe, has run a professional school for chefs. Green shrimp are shrimp with the heads still on.

- ¾ cup unsalted butter
- 2 packages (10 oz each) frozen okra, thawed and thinly sliced
- ¾ cup chopped onion
- ½ cup finely chopped green pepper
- 2 tablespoons finely minced garlic
- 2 tablespoons flour
- 4 cups chicken stock
- 2 to 3 cups peeled, coarsely chopped tomatoes
- ½ teaspoon dried thyme
- 1 teaspoon salt
  White pepper to taste
  Tomato paste (optional)
- 2 pounds green shrimp
- ½ pound crabmeat
- 2 tablespoons lemon juice
- 2 teaspoons Worcestershire sauce
- ¼ teaspoon hot-pepper sauce
  Cayenne pepper (optional)

1. Melt ¼ cup of the butter in a 12-inch skillet over medium heat. Add okra and cook, stirring constantly, until okra stops "roping," or until the white threads of the vegetable, which act as a thickener, disappear. Set aside.

2. In a large pot melt the remaining ½ cup butter over moderate heat and add onion, green pepper, and garlic. Cook over low heat for 10 minutes. Add flour. After flour is absorbed cook for 2 to 3 minutes.

3. Stirring constantly, add chicken stock. When the mixture has blended, add okra, tomato, thyme, salt, and pepper. Bring to a boil, reduce heat as low as possible, and simmer, partially covered, for 30 minutes.

4. If necessary, correct color by adding tomato paste (see Note). Add shrimp and simmer until full color has developed, 5 to 7 minutes. Add crab. When heated add lemon juice, Worcestershire, and hot-pepper sauce. Correct seasonings. Add cayenne, if desired.

Serves 8 to 10.

Note The sauce should be a rich, red color. If it is not red enough, you may heighten the color before adding the shrimp. To do this, dilute about 3 tablespoons of tomato paste with some of the stock, then add to the mixture in the pan. If more color is needed, add 2 additional tablespoons of tomato paste in the same manner.

OYSTERS AND EGGS

Kass Kapsiak, an energetic lady from a long line of Italian cooks, created this quick, easy, and delicious egg dish. Use Camembert made from goat milk if you prefer a more robust flavor. Serve with English muffins.

- ¼ cup unsalted butter
- 2 cloves garlic, pressed
- 1 cup sliced mushrooms
- 1 jar (8 oz) oysters, drained (cut large oysters in half)
- 2 green onions, chopped (include part of green)
- 4 eggs, lightly beaten
- 2 to 3 ounces Camembert cheese

1. Melt butter in a large skillet; add garlic and mushrooms. Sauté for about 4 minutes. Add oysters and onion and sauté for 4 more minutes.

2. Add beaten eggs and tilt skillet so that the egg covers the mixture. Add chunks of cheese and continue to cook over moderate heat. If the top of the mixture remains wet, briefly brown the top under the broiler.

3. Slip out of the pan onto a plate or invert onto a plate. Cut into pie-shaped wedges to serve.

Serves 4 to 6.

BOUILLABAISSE À LA MARSEILLES

This wonderful fish and shellfish creation has many different interpretations. Leave shellfish in their shells for extra flavor.

- 1 cup chopped white onion
- 2 leeks, white part only, chopped
- 1½ cups peeled, seeded, chopped tomato
- 2 cloves garlic, minced
- 3 tablespoons minced Italian parsley
- 2 to 3 sprigs fresh fennel
- 1 teaspoon salt
- ½ teaspoon pepper
- 8 pounds fish and shellfish, cleaned and trimmed
- 1 lobster, split

- 8 cups Fish Fumet (see page 17)
- 1 loaf French bread, sliced
- 1 recipe Rouille Sauce (see page 89)

In a large pot place onion, leek, tomato, garlic, parsley, and fennel. Sprinkle with salt and pepper. Lay pieces of firm fish on top of vegetables. Place lobster on top, cut side down. Pour fumet over top; simmer, covered, for 15 minutes. Add prawns and delicate fish and shellfish and simmer for 3 minutes. Strain and place fish and shellfish on serving plate. Serve broth over slice of French bread and add a spoonful of Rouille.

Serves 10 to 12.

Visual appeal can be just as important to your dinner guests as delicately balanced flavors. This study in green and white, a variation of Salade de Saint-Jacques, combines scallops, enoki mushrooms, watercress, and asparagus in a striking pattern. Guests will be eager to taste such a creation.

OVEN-STEAMED REDFISH WITH OYSTERS AND MUSHROOMS

Bruce Aidells has a champion sausage-making business. He is also a proponent and teacher of Cajun cookery. This classic Louisiana recipe uses Gulf Coast redfish, but you may use rock cod, halibut, or sea bass.

- ½ teaspoon dried tarragon
- ½ teaspoon dried whole oregano leaves
- ¼ teaspoon cayenne pepper
- 1 teaspoon paprika
- ½ teaspoon salt
- ½ teaspoon pepper
- 4 redfish fillets (6 to 8 oz each)
  Juice of 1 lemon
- 2 tablespoons unsalted butter
- ¼ pound mushrooms, thinly sliced
- 1 clove garlic
- 1 jar (10 oz) small oysters
- ½ cup whipping cream
  Salt and pepper to taste
  Lemon slices (for garnish)

1. Preheat oven to 400° F. Make a spice mixture by combining tarragon, oregano, cayenne, paprika, the ½ teaspoon salt, and the ½ teaspoon pepper in a small bowl. Rub both sides of fish with spiced mixture and half the lemon juice. Set aside.

2. In a small sauté pan, melt butter and sauté mushrooms and garlic for 2 to 3 minutes. Add remaining lemon juice and oysters; cook for 1 minute. Season with salt and pepper to taste and remove oysters and mushrooms. Reserve the liquid in the pan.

3. Place fillets in a roasting pan and cover with oyster-mushroom mixture. Cover the pan tightly with foil and steam in the oven until just done, 10 to 15 minutes. Remove fillets and oyster-mushroom topping to a warm place. Reserve juices in roasting pan.

4. To prepare sauce, add the juices in the roasting pan to reserved oyster-mushroom liquid. Add cream and reduce sauce over medium heat until just thick enough to coat a spoon.

Season sauce with salt, pepper, and lemon juice if needed. Pour over the fish, oysters, and mushrooms. Garnish with lemon slices.

Serves 4.

GOUJONNETTES DE SOLES AUX PÂTES FRAÎCHES
Sole twists with fresh pasta

Marc Halperin, a confirmed Francophile, lived and worked in France. His excellent training is reflected in this beautiful pasta dish. Gudgeons (*goujons* in French) are European freshwater finger-length fish. In this recipe, strips of sole are twisted and sautéed to resemble actual gudgeons.

- 16 ounces sole fillets
  Salt and pepper
  Flour for dredging
- 3 tablespoons unsalted butter
- 3 tablespoons vegetable oil
- 10 ounces fresh fettucine
- ½ cup whipping cream
- 2 tablespoons fines herbes

Vin Blanc Sauce

- 2 cups Fish Fumet (page 17)
- 1 large shallot, finely chopped
- ½ cup white wine
- ¼ cup dry vermouth
- ½ cup unsalted butter, cut in pieces
  Salt and pepper to taste
- 2 tablespoons lemon juice

1. Prepare Vin Blanc Sauce. Cut fish into strips ½ inch by 2 inches. Season with salt and pepper. Roll fish in flour, brushing off excess. Twist ends in opposite directions, like a candy wrapper. In medium sauté pan heat butter and oil. Sauté fish until golden. Drain and keep warm.

2. Cook fettucine in large pot of boiling salted water until al dente or just barely tender. Drain. In medium pan bring cream to boil, add fettucine, and season with salt and pepper to taste. Toss well.

3. Place fettucine on serving platter, scatter fish on top. Cover fish with some sauce and serve the rest on the side. Sprinkle with fines herbes and serve immediately.

Serves 4.

Vin Blanc Sauce In a medium pan combine fumet, shallot, wine, and vermouth. Reduce until syrupy. Whisk in butter bit by bit. Season with salt, pepper, and lemon juice. Keep warm but not hot.

FLAMING BANANA BASS

Betty Jewett Miller, a highly innovative cook, contributed this unusual and delicious recipe of her grandmother's.

- ⅔ cup whipping cream
- 2 sea bass fillets (8 oz each; 1 in. thick)
  Salt and freshly ground white pepper
  Half a large, ripe banana, mashed
- 2 tablespoons unsalted butter, melted
- 4 tablespoons shredded Gruyère cheese
- 4 tablespoons grated Parmesan cheese
- 2 tablespoons Cognac or whiskey

1. Preheat oven to 425° F. Place cream in a small pan and reduce over high heat until 2 to 3 tablespoons remain.

2. Place fish in a small, buttered casserole. Sprinkle with salt and pepper, then cover with banana, reduced cream, melted butter, Gruyère, and Parmesan. Bake 10 to 15 minutes; cooking time depends on size of fish.

3. In very small pan or ladle, heat Cognac or whiskey. Remove casserole from oven and pour warm liquor over the fish. Ignite with match. When flames die, serve immediately.

Serves 4 to 6.

CRAB CIOPPINO

The coastal town of Half Moon Bay, 30 minutes south of San Francisco, is famous as the "Pumpkin Capital of the World," and for the fresh Dungeness crab available there. The San Benito House, a restored turn-of-the-century country inn, provides excellent accommodations and wonderful meals. Carol Mickelsen, owner and executive chef, shares this special regional recipe. Substitute clam juice for the fish stock, if you wish.

- 3 tablespoons olive oil
- ½ cup chopped green onion (white part only)
- 6 shallots, minced
- 5 large tomatoes, peeled, seeded, and chopped
- 2 large cloves garlic, finely minced
- 3 tablespoons chopped Italian parsley
- 2 tablespoons chopped fresh dill, oregano, or fennel
- 1 bay leaf
- 4 tablespoons tomato paste (optional)
- 4 to 6 fresh Dungeness crabs
  Salt and freshly ground pepper to taste

San Benito House Fish Stock

- 2 pounds non-oily fish bones and shells
- 2 cups water
- 2 cups white wine
- 6 parsley stems
- 1 bay leaf
- ½ cup chopped celery leaves

1. In large pot heat oil and sauté onion until transparent. Add shallots, tomatoes, garlic, parsley, dill, and bay leaf. Simmer over very low heat for 15 minutes. Evaluate flavor and body halfway through cooking; add tomato paste if broth is very thin. Add San Benito House Fish Stock and continue simmering another 30 minutes. Do not cover.

2. Meanwhile, bring large pot of water to a full boil, add crabs, and cook for 14 minutes. Remove crabs immediately. Crabs should be slightly undercooked. When cool enough to handle, remove claws, legs, and backs. Work over a bowl to catch crab juices. Break bodies in half. Do not wash crabs. Stir crab juices into tomato sauce. Cook 10 to 15 minutes, then add salt and pepper.

3. Crack crab pieces by pounding them gently with a mallet. Add them to sauce and simmer for another 5 to 8 minutes.

Serves 6 to 8.

San Benito House Fish Stock In a large kettle combine fish bones and shells, water, wine, parsley, bay leaf, and celery leaves and bring to a boil. Skim off scum that appears on the surface. Simmer, uncovered, for 30 to 45 minutes. Strain. May be refrigerated for up to 2 days.

Makes 4 cups.

Crab Cioppino celebrates the delicious West Coast favorite, Dungeness crab, although other types of crab may be substituted. Serve this hearty dish with French bread and butter.

FISH IN MOROCCAN CHARMOULA SAUCE

Joyce Goldstein has been an inspiration to many through her cooking school (one of the first in San Francisco), her work at Chez Panisse in Berkeley, and at her own restaurant, Square One in San Francisco. Her dedication to wonderful foods shows with this recipe.

> 3 pounds firm fish fillets
> 4 potatoes, roasted and sliced
> 2 green peppers, sliced and sautéed briefly
> 2 tomatoes, sliced
> Salt and pepper to taste
> 1 lemon

Charmoula Sauce

> ½ cup chopped cilantro
> ½ cup chopped parsley
> 5 cloves garlic, finely chopped
> 5 tablespoons lemon juice
> 1½ teaspoons salt
> 1 teaspoon paprika
> ⅓ teaspoon ground cumin
> Cayenne pepper to taste
> ½ cup or more olive oil

1. Preheat oven to 425° F. Prepare Charmoula Sauce. Place fillets on bed of roasted potatoes, sautéed green peppers, and sliced tomatoes in a 13-by 9-inch pan. Salt and pepper fish, top with Charmoula Sauce. Add a squeeze of lemon.

2. Bake until fish is done (10 to 15 minutes, depending upon size of fish).

Serves 6 to 8.

Charmoula Sauce Combine cilantro, parsley, garlic, lemon juice, salt, paprika, cumin, and cayenne. Add enough olive oil to make thick sauce.

Note Fish can also be marinated in this sauce, then baked or grilled. Baste the fish with the sauce.

RED SNAPPER IN FILO

Gabby Saylor is an energetic woman who owns and operates a large catering business. This adaptation of *coulibiac* using filo is an example of her creativity.

> 2 packages (10 oz each) frozen leaf spinach
> 1 cup clarified butter, melted (see page 114)
> ½ pound mushrooms, sliced
> 1 teaspoon dried rosemary
> Salt and pepper to taste
> 2 pounds red snapper fillets
> 16 sheets filo dough
> 2 cups cooked saffron rice (rice cooked in a conventional manner with a pinch of saffron)

Lemon Butter Sauce

> 2 tablespoons lemon juice
> 1 tablespoon water
> Salt and pepper to taste
> 1 cup unsalted butter, melted

1. Defrost spinach and drain. In a medium saucepan melt 1 tablespoon of the clarified butter, add mushrooms and spinach; cook until most of the liquid has disappeared. Add rosemary, salt, and pepper, and continue to cook until all liquid has evaporated. Let cool.

2. Cut each piece of fish into a rectangle weighing approximately ¼ pound. (You should have 8 pieces.)

3. Preheat oven to 400° F. Brush one sheet of filo with a little of the clarified butter. Lay the next piece on top and brush with more butter. Place about ¼ cup saffron rice in a rectangle on the filo. Place a rectangle of

fish on top of this and salt and pepper generously. On top of this place ¼ cup of spinach-mushroom mixture. Making a package, turn the ends of filo on three sides around the fish, brush with more butter, and roll closed. Repeat with remaining ingredients. Place on ungreased cookie sheet. The packages may be refrigerated for a few hours.

4. Prior to cooking, brush with more melted butter. Bake until golden brown, about 15 minutes. Serve with Lemon Butter Sauce on the side.

Serves 8.

Lemon Butter Sauce In a small dish combine lemon juice, water, salt, pepper, and butter. Mix well.

SHRIMP MARSALA

Charlotte Walker has worked with equal success as a food consultant, author, lecturer, and food stylist. Simplicity contributes greatly to the success of this recipe.

> 1½ pounds Argentine pink shrimp or regular shrimp
> 6 tablespoons unsalted butter
> 2 tablespoons finely chopped shallot or white portion of green onion
> ½ pound small mushrooms, sliced
> ¾ cup whipping cream
> 3 to 4 tablespoons Marsala or Madeira wine
> Salt and white pepper to taste
> Finely chopped fresh chives, chervil, or parsley

1. Shell and devein shrimp. Pat dry with paper towels. Melt 3 tablespoons of the butter in a large skillet over medium heat. Add shallot and mushrooms; sauté about 2 minutes. Spoon into a medium bowl, and set aside. Reserve juices in skillet.

2. Melt the remaining 3 tablespoons butter in a medium skillet. Add shrimp and sauté until shrimp are firm and opaque, about 2½ minutes. Using a slotted spoon add shrimp to mushroom mixture. Add cream and wine to juices in the skillet used to cook shrimp. Add any juices that remain in the large skillet. Cook over medium-high heat until sauce is reduced to ⅔ to ¾ cup and thickens just enough to lightly coat a spoon. Add reserved mushrooms and shrimp; cook to heat through. Season with salt and white pepper to taste. Sprinkle with chives, chervil, or parsley.

Serves 4.

MOULES MARINIÈRE

Kittina Powers teaches classes in French and Mediterranean seasonal foods. Well known as an excellent teacher and lecturer, she places emphasis on high quality and fresh ingredients.

  6 *dozen mussels*
  4 *shallots, chopped*
  1 *bay leaf*
  ½ *teaspoon fennel seed*
  1 *cup dry white wine*
  1 *cup whipping cream*
  3 *egg yolks*
     Juice of 1 lemon
  2 *tablespoons unsalted butter*
     Salt and pepper
     Chopped parsley

1. Scrub and debeard mussels. Soak them in a bowl of cold water or in sink for 30 minutes. Any sand will leach out and sink to the bottom of the bowl.

2. In a large stockpot, simmer shallots, bay leaf, fennel seed, and wine for 5 minutes. Add mussels and steam for 5 minutes; all mussels should open in that time. If doubling recipe, it will take longer for mussels to open. Transfer mussels to a large bowl and keep them warm.

3. To make sauce, strain mussel stock and boil until reduced to about 1½ cups. In a medium bowl beat together cream, egg yolks, and lemon juice. Add 1 cup of mussel stock to cream and eggs in a thin stream, then pour the whole lot back into the stock. Heat very gently, stirring all the while so that egg yolks do not scramble. Turn off the heat and stir in butter. Season with salt and pepper, if necessary.

4. Divide mussels among 6 large, shallow soup bowls. Ladle sauce over each bowl and sprinkle each with chopped parsley. Place a large bowl on the table for mussel shells.

Serves 6.

Moules Marinière is an adaptation of a classic French dish that never fails to please even the most discriminating palate. Easily prepared and economical, this recipe may well become a mainstay in your seafood repertoire.

Scallops are perfect for simple but elegant entertaining. They require very little preparation and they can be combined with a wide variety of vegetables and sauces, creating infinite possibilities. If you like creating recipes, try combining scallops with any of the many sauce recipes on pages 114–122.

BAY SCALLOPS WITH GINGER-LIME BEURRE BLANC

This recipe comes from Christian Iser, executive chef at the Stanford Court Hotel in San Francisco, which has one of the most famous hotel kitchens in the country.

    2 tablespoons chopped shallot
    1 teaspoon grated fresh ginger
       Juice of 2 limes
    1 tablespoon white wine vinegar
    1 tablespoon dry white wine
    2 cups unsalted butter, at room temperature
    1 pound bay scallops
    ¼ cup chopped chives
    1 lime, cut in slender wedges (for garnish)
    5 sprigs parsley (for garnish)

1. In a small saucepan combine shallot, ginger, lime juice, vinegar, and wine. Boil mixture over high heat until almost dry.

2. Add all except 2 tablespoons butter to mixture, 1 to 2 tablespoons at a time. Whisk well after each addition. The mixture should look creamy and white. Reserve over very low heat.

3. In a medium sauté pan, heat the remaining 2 tablespoons butter. Add scallops and sauté very quickly; scallops should be underdone. Drain and add to sauce.

4. Place scallops with sauce in middle of each plate. Sprinkle chives over the top. Garnish with lime wedges and a sprig of parsley.

Serves 5.

FISH IN PUFF PASTRY

Jim Dodge is the star in the pastry kitchen at San Francisco's Stanford Court Hotel. Besides sweet pastry, he also takes a turn at savories. This New England recipe comes from the Dodge family tradition of hotel and restaurant expertise.

1½ pounds Pacific snapper or
*   salmon (1½-inch-thick fillets)*
3 sprigs fresh marjoram
*   Juice of half a medium-*
*   sized lemon*
½ cup unsalted butter
3 whole peppercorns
1½ cups Fish Fumet (page 17)
*   or clam juice*
1 cup Fumé Blanc or other
*   dry white wine*
¼ cup flour
17 ounces puff pastry dough
1 large egg, beaten

1. Preheat oven to 550° F. Place fish on buttered baking sheet with a rim. Remove the leaves from 1 sprig of the marjoram and mince. Sprinkle over fish. Pour lemon juice over fish, then dot with ¼ cup of the butter. Bake until fish is half cooked, about 5 minutes.

2. Place a wire rack on top of another baking sheet, and place a piece of waxed or parchment paper on top of the rack. Carefully remove fish from other baking sheet and place on paper. This will allow the juices to drain off. Allow fish to cool completely.

3. Reduce oven to 450° F. Prepare sauce in a 2-quart saucepan by combining peppercorns, Fish Fumet, wine, and remaining 2 sprigs of the marjoram. Bring to a boil. In another small pan, melt remaining ¼ cup butter. Add flour, and whisk until smooth. Add butter-flour mixture to fumet mixture, stirring continuously until dissolved. Simmer 45 minutes in oven.

4. Cut puff pastry in half and roll each piece into a 12- by 18-inch rectangle, ¼ inch thick. Cut out two 12- by 18-inch teardrop shapes. Place one on a baking sheet lined with parchment paper. Brush edges with beaten egg. Place fish in the center of dough. Cover with the second piece of dough, pressing the edges to seal.

5. Brush top of dough with beaten egg. Form leftover dough to resemble an eye, a fin, and a tail. Use scissors to cut small V-shaped cuts through the dough to resemble scales. The cuts will also allow steam to escape. Bake at 450° F until golden brown, 30 to 40 minutes. Pour remaining juices into sauce. Strain sauce and serve with fish.

Serves 2.

SEAFOOD SHORTCAKE

Steven Froman is the talented pastry chef at the Campton Place Hotel in San Francisco. It is his belief that one can have a sense of humor about food, so he created this seafood shortcake as a savory counterpart to the famous dessert.

4 pieces sea urchin roe (see Note)
1½ cups whipping cream
2 tablespoons clarified butter
*   (see page 114)*
8 ounces assorted seafood—
*   lobster, shrimp, crab, scallops,*
*   small pieces of fish, mussels,*
*   crayfish*
1 teaspoon minced shallot
¼ cup dry vermouth
*   Salt and pepper to taste*
1 teaspoon chopped fresh
*   marjoram*
*   Pinch cayenne pepper*

Shortcake

2 cups flour
¾ teaspoon salt
2 teaspoons baking powder
2 teaspoons sugar
1 tablespoon chopped fresh
*   marjoram*
¼ cup unsalted butter
1 cup whipping cream

1. Prepare Shortcake. To prepare seafood, place roe in a small bowl. Add cream slowly, stirring constantly. In medium pan melt butter and sauté seafood; add the longer-cooking elements to the pan first. Remove seafood when almost done. Add shallot, sauté until soft, about 1 minute. Add vermouth, reduce the liquid by one half, then add cream mixture, salt, pepper, marjoram, and cayenne. Reduce slightly to thicken.

2. Split baked shortcakes in half and place the bottoms on warm serving plates. Return seafood to sauce to warm. Place sauce and seafood on each shortcake bottom, letting some spill over onto the plate. Pour the remaining sauce over and around the cakes. Top each serving with the remaining shortcake rounds, leaving them slightly askew to expose seafood and sauce. Serve immediately.

Serves 8.

Note If the roe is unavailable, substitute 1 beaten egg yolk. After the sauce has thickened, remove from heat, and slowly beat the yolk into the sauce. Return sauce to heat. (Do not let sauce boil after adding yolk.)

Shortcake Preheat oven to 350° F. Mix flour, salt, baking powder, sugar; then sift. Add marjoram. Roll butter and dry ingredients between thumbs and forefingers to create pea-sized pieces. Add cream and mix carefully into a dough. Do not overmix. Use more flour to avoid sticking. Roll out to about ⅜ inch thick and cut into eight 3-inch circles. Score the tops of the circles and cut the edges to achieve a scallop effect. Bake until golden brown, 10 to 12 minutes.

SHRIMP WITH SNOW PEAS AND MELON

Michelle Schmidt is an accomplished cookbook author and food consultant and is well known for her skills in recipe and product development.

> 1 pound medium shrimp
> Juice of 2 limes
> 3 tablespoons thin soy sauce
> ⅛ teaspoon red pepper flakes
> ⅓ pound snow peas
> One 1-inch piece fresh ginger
> 4 slices prosciutto
> 3 tablespoons safflower oil
> 1 small cantaloupe

1. Choose a saucepan large enough to accommodate shrimp. Fill halfway with hot tap water. Add shrimp and bring to a boil; simmer for 1 minute—do not cook longer. Plunge shrimp into ice water, then peel, and cut in half lengthwise. Rinse and devein under cool running water. Dry and reserve.

2. Mix lime juice with soy sauce and pepper flakes. Marinate shrimp in this mixture in refrigerator for at least 3 hours but not longer than 6 hours.

3. Break tips off snow peas and remove strings. Blanch in boiling salted water and plunge into ice water. Drain and cut lengthwise into julienne. Reserve. Peel ginger, slice paper-thin, then cut into fine julienne. Reserve. Trim fat from prosciutto and cut into fine julienne.

4. Before serving, drain shrimp and reserve 1 tablespoon of marinade. Mix shrimp, snow peas, ginger, and prosciutto. Blend reserved marinade with oil and toss with shrimp mixture. Cut four rings about ⅜ inch thick from center of melon. Seed and peel. Place one on each of 4 plates. Mound one fourth of the shrimp mixture in each melon ring.

Serves 4.

SHRIMP À LA GRECQUE

Ruth Robinson is a manufacturer of varietal vinegars and a bottler of wonderful California olive oils. She adapted this recipe from one created by Marti Sousanis, a specialist in Middle Eastern foods. It is a combination of shrimp, feta cheese, and ouzo, an anise-flavored liquor much favored in Middle Eastern cooking.

> 6 tablespoons olive oil
> 1 medium onion, chopped
> 4 cloves garlic, peeled and chopped
> 6 to 8 fresh tomatoes
> Salt and pepper to taste
> 2 tablespoons unsalted butter
> 2 pounds shrimp, shelled and deveined
> 2 tablespoons Cognac
> 2 tablespoons ouzo
> ¼ pound feta cheese, diced
> 2 tablespoons parsley, chopped

1. Heat 4 tablespoons of the olive oil in a medium pan. Add onion and garlic, and cook until lightly browned. Add tomatoes, salt, and pepper. Cook over low heat until mixture thickens.

2. Preheat oven to 425° F. In a medium pan heat remaining 2 tablespoons olive oil and butter. Sauté shrimp until they turn pink, about 2 minutes. In a very small pan or ladle, heat Cognac. Pour ouzo and Cognac over shrimp and ignite. When flames die, place shrimp in casserole, cover with tomato mixture then with cheese. Sprinkle with parsley and bake about 10 minutes.

Serves 8.

SCALLOP AND FISH TARTARE

This version of the classic beef dish, Steak Tartare, has the fresh taste of the sea. Do not put fish in the food processor or it will be mushy and the dish will not have the proper consistency. Scallop and Fish Tartare is a wonderful appetizer, first course, or main dish for a light luncheon.

> ½ cup olive oil
> ½ cup vegetable oil
> 1 egg yolk
> 1 tablespoon white wine vinegar
> ½ teaspoon kosher salt
> ¼ teaspoon white pepper
> ½ pound sea scallops
> 2 pounds sea bass fillets
> 2 teaspoons Dijon mustard
> 2 teaspoons minced shallot
> ¼ teaspoon Worcestershire sauce
> 2 ounces caviar
> Baby lettuce leaves
> 2 tablespoons chopped chives
> Lemon juice to taste

1. In a small bowl combine olive oil and vegetable oil. Set aside. In a food processor fitted with steel blade, process egg yolk, vinegar, salt, and pepper for 5 seconds. With machine running, add oils in a slow, steady stream until mayonnaise forms. Reserve.

2. With a very sharp knife, chop scallops and bass together until they are a very fine mixture. Combine with mustard, shallot, Worcestershire sauce, and ½ cup of the mayonnaise to form tartar mixture. Reserve remaining mayonnaise for other dishes.

3. Divide tartar mixture into 8 individual portions and scoop onto small serving plates. Push half an eggshell filled with caviar down into the center of each scoop. Place baby lettuce leaves to the side. Scatter chives over tartar, sprinkle with lemon juice, and serve immediately.

Serves 8.

CALAMARI SALAD WITH DILL-PARSLEY VINAIGRETTE

Marlene Levinson, a San Francisco cooking instructor and well-known food maven, is also known for her creativity and expertise in the wholesale salad business. This is sure to delight calamari lovers.

- 3 pounds calamari, cleaned and cut in ringlets
- 2 to 3 ribs celery, thinly sliced
- 6 green onions, thinly sliced

Dill-Parsley Vinaigrette

- 1 teaspoon chopped fresh dill
- ½ to ¾ cup chopped Italian parsley
- 3 tablespoons vegetable oil
- ½ cup red wine vinegar
  Salt and pepper to taste

1. Place calamari in a medium-sized pan. Cover with heavily salted water. Slowly, while stirring constantly, bring water to a near boil. Calamari should, at that point, be cooked.

2. Remove from heat and rinse immediately under cold water.

3. Combine with celery and green onion. Marinate in Dill-Parsley Vinaigrette for at least 1 hour. Correct seasoning by adding salt, pepper, and vinegar if necessary.

Serves 4 to 6.

Dill-Parsley Vinaigrette Mix dill, parsley, oil, vinegar, salt, and pepper.

ROQUEFORT PRAWNS

Kathryn Mayerhofer is a caterer and free-lance cooking teacher in the San Francisco Bay Area. She studied at Le Cordon Bleu in Paris and trained in chocolates and pastries in Germany.

- 2 pounds prawns
- 5 tablespoons unsalted butter
- ⅔ cup dry white wine
- ⅓ pound Roquefort cheese
- ½ cup finely minced parsley (for garnish)

1. Shell and devein prawns. Rinse in cold water. In a large sauté pan, melt butter over medium heat. Add prawns and sauté until just done, 2 to 3 minutes.

2. Remove prawns from pan, keep warm. Deglaze pan by adding wine and scraping bottom of pan to dissolve the flavorful particles.

3. Crumble cheese and add to pan slowly, stirring constantly. When cheese is melted, add prawns and reheat. Remove from pan and garnish with parsley.

Serves 6 to 8.

Colorful Shrimp With Snow Peas and Melon makes a lovely luncheon entrée or first course for dinner. The marinated shrimp can be made ahead and the salad assembled just before serving.

Any white-fleshed fish can be substituted in the wonderful combination of flavors and colors of Sea Bass With Mexican Salsa.

SALMON AND SCALLOPS IN PUFF PASTRY

Gary Jenanyan is a superb classical chef who studied with the great chefs of Europe.

1½	*pounds puff pastry*
4	*ounces smoked salmon, thinly sliced*
12	*ounces salmon fillet*
30	*fresh baby bay or calico scallops*
1½	*pounds scallops*
1	*bunch sorrel*
1	*cup good-quality dry white wine*
1	*cup dry vermouth*
5	*shallots, thinly sliced*
4	*cups whipping cream*
3	*shallots, finely minced*
	Salt and pepper
2	*whole eggs*
1	*teaspoon whipping cream*
½	*teaspoon water*

1. *To prepare pastry:* Roll puff pastry ⅛ inch thick and cut into twelve 5-inch squares. Refrigerate. Cut 6 pieces of smoked salmon into 2½-inch squares no thicker than ³⁄₁₆ inch. Refrigerate. Cut 6 pieces of salmon fillet into 2½-inch squares no thicker than ½ inch. Refrigerate.

2. *To prepare scallops:* Keeping the two quantities of scallops separate, clean all of the scallops; remove membrane if necessary. Wash and stem sorrel; dry very thoroughly. Roll sorrel in a tight roll and cut into a fine chiffonade (fine strips or ribbons).

3. *To prepare sauce:* In a 4-quart heavy-bottomed saucepan place wine, vermouth, and the 1½ pounds scallops. Simmer slowly for 40 minutes. Strain out scallops and discard them. Return broth to saucepan, add the 5 sliced shallots, and reduce to a glaze (thick syrup); do not burn. Stir in the 4 cups cream and simmer to desired consistency. Remove from heat, strain out shallots, and return sauce to a clean, heavy-bottomed pan. Set aside.

4. *To assemble:* Preheat oven to 425° F. Working quickly, remove 2 puff pastry squares at a time from the refrigerator. With a fork prick a 2-inch square in the center of each square as you would prick a pie crust. In the center of each pastry square, place a slice of smoked salmon, then add a piece of salmon fillet, and a teaspoon of the minced shallot. Salt and pepper generously, then top each square with 1 heaping tablespoon of sorrel chiffonade and 5 of the baby bay scallops.

5. With fingertips, carefully spread a few drops of water on the edges around the filling. Cover each mound of ingredients carefully with a square of pastry. Seal the seams thoroughly, removing as much air as possible. With a sharp knife, square the edges, leaving a 1-inch border. Decorate the borders as you wish. Cut a small steam hole in the center of each top. Refrigerate and repeat until all have been completed.

6. Prepare an egg wash by mixing eggs, the 1 teaspoon whipping cream, and the water in a saucer. Paint the top of each square with the wash. Refrigerate.

7. *Just before serving:* Reheat sauce over low heat. Season to taste with salt and pepper and keep warm.

8. Remove pastries from refrigerator, paint a second time with egg wash, and place on a heavy baking sheet. Bake until pastry is golden brown, 12 to 15 minutes. Do not overcook.

9. Place about ⅓ cup of sauce in the center of 6 warm plates. Place pastries on the sauce, and serve as soon as possible.

Serves 6 as a first course for dinner or as a main course for lunch.

SEA BASS WITH MEXICAN SALSA

Gayle Henderson Wilson is a food consultant who specializes in recipe development and food research. She is a past president of the San Francisco Professional Food Society.

> 1 pound tomatoes, peeled and chopped or 1¾ cups (28-oz can) crushed tomatoes with purée
> 1 cup (4-oz can) olive wedges, drained
> ½ cup diced English (hothouse) cucumber
> ⅓ cup chopped green onion
> 1 tablespoon minced serrano chile or any hot chile
> 1 tablespoon minced cilantro
> 3 tablespoons olive oil
> 1 tablespoon red wine vinegar
> 1 teaspoon minced garlic
> ¾ teaspoon kosher salt
> 8 dashes hot-pepper sauce, or to taste
> Pinch freshly ground black pepper
> 1¾ pounds sea bass

1. Prepare a marinade in a large glass or ceramic bowl by mixing tomatoes, olive wedges, cucumber, onion, chile, and cilantro.

2. Stir in oil, vinegar, garlic, salt, hot-pepper sauce, and black pepper. Set aside for several hours or refrigerate overnight for flavors to blend.

3. Prepare coals on barbecue or preheat oven to 375° F. Lay out two pieces of heavy-duty aluminum foil, one on top of the other, crosswise.

4. Place fish on top of the foil and cover with marinade. Make a note of how thick the fish is; this will determine cooking time. Bring four corners of foil together to form a tightly closed packet; juices should not spill out. Leave space between the closure of the package and the fish. If fish is in 2 large pieces, prepare 2 packages, and split the marinade between them.

5. Bake in oven or over moderate coals. Allow 10 to 12 minutes cooking time for each inch of thickness of the fish.

6. Open package and serve fish covered with sauce on warm plates.

Serves 4.

LEMON PASTA WITH MUSSELS

Connie McCole is a San Francisco cooking teacher. She has studied extensively with the great teachers of Italian cuisine in this country and in Europe, and this recipe reflects her training.

> 4 pounds mussels, in the shell
> 1½ cups dry white wine
> 6 tablespoons unsalted butter
> 2 tablespoons olive oil
> 4 cloves garlic, minced
> ¼ cup minced parsley
> Freshly ground black pepper to taste
> 1 cup whipping cream
> 2 tablespoons unsalted butter
> Salt to taste

Three-Egg Lemon Pasta

> 2 to 2¼ cups flour
> 3 eggs, at room temperature
> 2 tablespoons lemon juice
> Grated rind of 2 large lemons
> ½ teaspoon salt

1. Wash and debeard mussels. Put mussels and wine in a large stockpot. Cover and turn heat to high. When mussels open, take them off the heat and remove from the pot with a slotted spoon, leaving behind as much broth as possible.

2. Remove mussels from shells. Strain the cooking broth through several thicknesses of cheesecloth. Reserve. Save a few shells for garnish. Chop mussels and set aside.

3. In a medium saucepan heat the 6 tablespoons butter and the olive oil with garlic. When garlic begins to soften, add parsley, pepper, strained broth, and cream. Let boil for 1 to 2 minutes. Stir in mussels until heated through, then remove from burner.

4. Add cooked pasta and the 2 tablespoons butter and toss gently to mix; salt to taste. Serve immediately.

Serves 6.

Three-Egg Lemon Pasta Place flour on work surface and make a well in the center. Break eggs into the well, add lemon juice, rind, and salt. Mix eggs and lemon juice with fork. Gradually add flour to liquid until a ball of dough is formed. Knead dough until it is a smooth, elastic ball, 5 to 8 minutes. Wrap dough in waxed paper and let rest for at least 30 minutes. Cut dough into linguine-shaped pasta. Bring 8 quarts of lightly salted water to a boil. Add pasta and cook until pasta rises to the top, about 30 seconds to 1 minute. Drain and use as directed in recipe.

CAVIAR

The word *caviar* conjures up the image of luxury. It is true that the finest caviar is among the most expensive foods, but there are many types that come at all price levels and offer great variety.

Sturgeon roe (eggs) comprises the very finest caviar. There are three major species of sturgeon: Beluga, Osetra, and Sevruga. The Beluga sturgeon, often reaching a length of 20 feet, is the largest and produces the largest eggs. Beluga caviar is the most expensive. The eggs vary in color from dark, steely gray to light gray. The next largest and expensive is the Osetra. Averaging 6 to 7 feet long, the Osetra produces eggs that range in color from dark gray to gray with a golden hue. Sevruga, the smallest of the sturgeon, rarely exceeds 4 feet. The least expensive of the major caviars, Sevruga eggs range from dark to medium gray.

These caviars set the standard for other caviars. Top-quality fresh sturgeon roe has a subtle, salty taste and does not taste fishy. The eggs are round, plump, and separate easily. The texture is soft but not mushy. The label *malossol* on these caviars means lightly salted and is indicative of a high-quality product. Sturgeon caviar should never be frozen. Refrigerated at 28° to 30° F, caviar in a tin will keep for about a month. Once opened and exposed to air, however, it will deteriorate rapidly, and quality is lost within a few hours.

Sturgeon are sea fish that come back to fresh water to spawn. Most of the sturgeon are caught in the deltas of rivers that flow into the Caspian Sea and the Black Sea. Thus, caviar usually comes from the Soviet Union, Iran, or Romania. Small amounts of American sturgeon caviar have appeared on the market, however.

Golden caviar is from the white-fish found in the Great Lakes. It is a little smaller than Sevruga caviar, is an attractive golden apricot to deep amber color, and has a clean, fresh taste. Like sturgeon roe, whitefish caviar must be kept under refrigeration, but unlike sturgeon, golden caviar may be frozen without loss of flavor and texture. In fact, it is often flash-frozen immediately after processing, which preserves the fresh taste. Thaw frozen caviar in the refrigerator, where it will keep up to a week and can be refrozen. Fresh and pasteurized golden caviars are also available in jars.

Salmon caviar is one of the largest roes prepared as caviar. The eggs have a pleasant taste and a distinct texture. They range in color from pale orange to bright red. Salmon caviar is available fresh in bulk or in jars in a pasteurized form.

Lumpfish caviar is usually imported from Iceland and sold in jars after pasteurization. It is dyed, and the color often runs, so this caviar benefits from rinsing to reduce the dye content as well as the salt, the taste of the preservative, and fishiness. To rinse, place caviar in a fine mesh strainer, and let cool water gently flow through for two to three minutes. Drain, cover, and chill thoroughly until ready to serve.

Other roes are beginning to find a place in the American market. The roe of the flying fish, which comes from Japan and is often found in sushi bars, is gaining popularity. It has a very crunchy texture and slightly fishy flavor. Crab roe has a more delicate crunchy texture and a bittersweet flavor. Flying fish and crab roes are lightly dyed to accentuate the natural colors, and are often sold frozen. Cod roe has an almost paste-like appearance and a fishy taste. Rinsing freshens the taste of all three of these roes.

Good caviar should be served chilled. Place it in a glass container on crushed ice to maintain freshness.

Served alone, caviar is a most exquisite hors d'oeuvre. It may also be served as a canapé on toast or blini. Spread the toast with a very thin layer of unsalted butter to keep the oils in the caviar from softening it.

Phil Quattrociocchi is a well-known West Coast importer of fine caviars. His favorite way to serve caviar is with an assortment of accompaniments: small bowls of chopped hard-boiled egg, minced green onion, toast points, and lemon wedges. The lemon is only needed if the caviar is too salty. Caviar in rolls of smoked salmon is also a favorite. Much of the popularity and quality of American golden caviar can be attributed to Mats and Dafne Engstrom, who were pioneers in the production of golden caviar in the United States. The care with which they process caviar is an important factor in the high quality of the finished product.

GOLDEN CAVIAR SAUCE

This recipe comes from Dafne Engstrom. It is extremely versatile and can be used as a dip for vegetables or as a wonderful sauce for fish or chicken.

> 4 *ounces golden caviar*
> ½ *cup vegetable oil*
> ½ *cup sour cream*
> 2 *tablespoons chopped chives or green top of green onion*
> ½ *teaspoon whole allspice, lightly crushed*
> 2 *teaspoons lemon juice*
> 2 *tablespoons vodka*
> 2 *teaspoons catsup*

1. Whisk the caviar in a medium bowl until it becomes frothy and the eggs begin to separate. Add oil slowly in a thin stream, whisking continually, until thoroughly incorporated. Fold in the sour cream.

2. Whisk in chives, allspice, lemon juice, vodka, and catsup. Serve at room temperature.

Makes about 1⅓ cups.

STEAMED MUSSELS WITH GOLDEN CAVIAR

Michael Nelson, well known for his interest in developing new and exciting products for American markets, developed this attractive presentation. In this dish he recommends the use of New Zealand green-lipped mussels. If these are unavailable, substitute another type of mussel, or you may use oysters or clams.

    3 pounds mussels
    ½ cup water
    1 cup sour cream or Lemon
      Crème Fraîche (see page 119)
    4 ounces golden caviar

1. Clean and debeard mussels, scrubbing the shells. Place mussels and the water in a large pot. Cover pot, and steam mussels over medium heat until shells open. Drain and let cool.

2. Open mussels, leaving mussel meat on the half shell. Arrange mussels attractively on platter. On each mussel place 1 heaping teaspoon of sour cream. Place ½ teaspoon golden caviar on top of sour cream.

Serves 6 to 8.

BLINI

Blini served with caviar are always popular. They may be made ahead of serving time.

    2 cups all-purpose flour
    ½ cup buckwheat flour
    1 package active dry yeast
    2 teaspoons sugar
    2 egg yolks
    3 cups lukewarm milk (100°
      to 105° F)
    3 egg whites
    2 tablespoons unsalted butter

1. In a medium bowl combine all-purpose and buckwheat flours. Stir in yeast and sugar. Make a well in flour and add egg yolks. Gradually stir in milk, incorporating yolks and flour.

2. Cover the bowl with a towel and place in a warm area. Let rise until doubled in bulk. Beat egg whites to soft peaks and fold into batter.

3. Melt butter on griddle or in large skillet. Form blini by dropping heaping tablespoons of batter onto hot griddle. Cook on both sides until golden brown.

Makes 2 dozen blini.

Caviars provide a touch of luxury, some at prices fit for a king. But there are many types of caviar and various ways to use it economically. Guests won't suspect that this bountiful caviar spread was in fact easy on the budget.

SAUCES

Though most fish and shellfish can be served with just a little butter and lemon, a sauce can transform the simplest dish into something quite special. Sauces here run the gamut from the simple to the sophisticated. Paying attention to ingredients and following the recipe will assure a grand result by even an inexperienced cook.

BEURRE ROUGE
Red butter sauce

⅔ cup red wine
3 shallots, finely minced
1 to 1½ cups unsalted butter, diced
Kosher salt and freshly ground white pepper

In a medium pan boil wine and shallots until shallots are barely moist. Remove pan from heat and let cool for a few minutes. Moving pan off and onto very low heat as needed, whisk in butter bit by bit until a creamy emulsion forms. Season with salt and pepper.

Makes about 1½ cups.

BEURRE BLANC
White butter sauce

⅓ cup dry white wine
⅓ cup white wine vinegar
3 shallots, finely minced
1 to 1½ cups unsalted butter, diced
Kosher salt and freshly ground white pepper

In a medium pan boil wine, vinegar, and shallots until shallots are barely moist. Remove pan from heat and let cool for a few minutes. Moving pan off and onto very low heat as needed, whisk in butter bit by bit until a creamy emulsion forms. Season with salt and pepper.

Makes 1½ cups.

CLARIFIED BUTTER

2 cups butter

In a heavy pan over low heat, melt butter. Skim off froth and carefully pour butter from pan, leaving the milky residue behind. Discard residue.

Makes about 1½ cups.

ROUX

Roux forms the base for many sauces. It must be heated gently to avoid a raw floury taste. The proportion of flour to butter determines the thickness of the roux, and thus of the sauce. This roux will make a medium cream sauce when added to 1 cup hot liquid. For a thicker sauce (used to prepare a soufflé), combine 3 tablespoons each butter and flour, to blend with 1 cup liquid.

2 tablespoons butter
2 tablespoons flour

In a small saucepan over medium-low heat, melt butter. Add flour and stir to blend; cook over low heat, stirring occasionally, 3 to 5 minutes.

Makes ¼ cup roux.

SAVORY BUTTERS

Known as Compound Butters, these butters have been softened, mixed with different herbs and flavorings, formed into a roll about 1 inch in diameter, and chilled. Cut off a slice whenever flavored butter is needed.

TOMATO BUTTER

2 tablespoons unsalted butter
1 medium tomato, seeded and chopped
1 shallot, minced
½ cup unsalted butter, softened

In a small sauté pan melt the 2 tablespoons butter, then add tomato and shallot. Cook until dry, then sieve. Blend with softened butter. Form into a cylinder and chill.

Makes ¾ cup.

FENNEL BUTTER

⅓ cup finely chopped fresh fennel
½ cup boiling water
½ cup unsalted butter, softened

Cook fennel in the boiling water for 1 minute. Drain and add to butter. Form into a cylinder and chill.

Makes ¾ cup.

RED PEPPER BUTTER

1 tablespoon unsalted butter
2 shallots, finely chopped
2 large red bell peppers, peeled, seeded, and finely chopped
1 tablespoon balsamic vinegar
½ cup unsalted butter, softened

In a small sauté pan, melt 1 tablespoon butter. Add shallots, red pepper, vinegar. Cook until peppers soften. Cool and add to softened butter. Form into a cylinder and chill.

Makes 1 cup.

PAPAYA BUTTER

1 tablespoon unsalted butter
1 large papaya, peeled, seeded, and chopped
3 tablespoons white wine
½ cup unsalted butter, softened

In a small pan melt the 1 tablespoon butter. Add papaya and white wine; cook until papaya is soft. Cool and mix with ½ cup softened butter. Form into a cylinder and chill.

Makes 1 cup.

ANCHOVY BUTTER

4 anchovy fillets
¼ cup milk
½ cup unsalted butter, softened

Place anchovy fillets in a small bowl and cover with milk. Let sit for 30 minutes; drain and discard milk. Mash and mix fillets with butter. Form into a cylinder and chill.

Makes ½ cup.

GARLIC BUTTER

5 cloves garlic, peeled
2 cups water
½ cup unsalted butter, softened

Place garlic in saucepan with the water. Bring to a boil and cook 5 minutes. Drain, cool, then crush garlic, and mix with butter. Form into a cylinder and chill.

Makes ½ cup.

LEMON BUTTER

Grated rind of 1 lemon
1 teaspoon lemon juice
½ cup unsalted butter, softened

Mix lemon rind and juice with butter. Form into a cylinder and chill.

Makes ½ cup.

HERB BUTTER

4 tablespoons of the herb of choice (thyme, tarragon, chives, oregano)
2 cups boiling water
½ cup unsalted butter, softened

Blanch herbs in the boiling water for 3 to 5 minutes. Drain, cool, and chop. Mix with butter. Form into a cylinder and chill.

Makes ½ cup.

SPRING BUTTER

½ cup green spring vegetable, such as peas, asparagus tips, or French green beans
2 cups boiling salted water
½ cup softened, unsalted butter

Drop cleaned vegetables into the boiling water. Cook until soft, drain, and sieve. Cool and mix with butter. Form into a cylinder and chill.

Makes 1 cup.

SHELLFISH BUTTER

½ pound crushed shrimp or crayfish or lobster shells
6 tablespoons unsalted butter
½ cup unsalted butter, softened

Pound crushed shells in mortar and pestle with the 6 tablespoons butter until almost smooth. Sieve and add to the ½ cup butter. Form into a cylinder and chill.

Makes ¾ cup.

MAÎTRE D'HÔTEL BUTTER

2 tablespoons chopped parsley
1 teaspoon lemon juice
½ cup unsalted butter, softened

Mix parsley, lemon juice, and butter. Form into a cylinder and chill.

Makes ½ cup.

If you just want to poach, sauté, or grill fresh fish or shellfish for a quick and simple dinner entrée, flavored butters add just the right seasoning and taste to turn it into something special. Spring Butter is flavored with a variety of vegetables, each providing a unique taste. Using unsalted butter as a base produces fresher taste.

An array of mayonnaises to enhance any food, clockwise from top: Red Pepper, With Nuts, Fines Herbes, Dill, Russian, Pesto, and, in the center, Mustard.

MAYONNAISES

Mayonnaise is a wonderful accompaniment that lends itself to many exciting variations. The food processor has reduced the time-consuming task of making mayonnaise by hand to a job that takes only minutes.

BASIC MAYONNAISE

- 1 whole egg
- 1 tablespoon lemon juice or wine vinegar
- 1 teaspoon kosher salt
- ¼ teaspoon freshly ground pepper
- 1½ cups oil

In a food processor fitted with steel blade, place egg, lemon juice, salt, and pepper. Process until blended, about 2 to 3 seconds. With machine running, pour oil through feed tube in a slow, steady stream. When thick, refrigerate. This mayonnaise will keep for 7 to 10 days.

Makes 1¾ cups.

PESTO MAYONNAISE

- 1 cup fresh basil leaves, tightly packed
- ¼ teaspoon salt
- 1 teaspoon minced garlic
- 1 tablespoon pine nuts
- ¼ cup grated Parmesan cheese
- ¼ teaspoon freshly ground black pepper
- ½ cup olive oil
- 1 cup Basic Mayonnaise (above)

To make pesto, in a food processor fitted with steel blade, process basil, salt, garlic, pine nuts, Parmesan, pepper, and olive oil until thick. Add 1 tablespoon of pesto mixture to mayonnaise; add more than 1 tablespoon to achieve a fuller flavor. Any remaining pesto may be frozen.

Makes 1 cup.

MAYONNAISE RAVIGOTE

- ¼ cup dry white wine
- 2 tablespoons chopped parsley
- 2 tablespoons drained, chopped capers
- 2 tablespoons minced onion
- 2 tablespoons minced shallot
- 2 tablespoons minced chives
- 1 cup Basic Mayonnaise (at left)
- ¼ teaspoon anchovy paste
- 1 hard-boiled egg white, minced
- 1 tablespoon lemon juice

In a small saucepan combine wine, parsley, capers, onion, shallot, and chives. Over high heat reduce to 1 tablespoon liquid. Remove from heat, and cool. In a small bowl combine mayonnaise, anchovy paste, egg white, and lemon juice. Add reduction and mix. Refrigerate and serve cold.

Makes 1¼ cups.

RED PEPPER MAYONNAISE

- 2 tablespoons oil
- 1 large shallot, peeled and minced
- 2 large red bell peppers, peeled, seeded, and chopped
- 1 cup Basic Mayonnaise (at left)

In a small sauté pan, heat oil. Add shallot and peppers; cook until shallot and peppers are soft. In a food processor fitted with steel blade, purée shallot and peppers. Add to mayonnaise. Chill and serve.

Makes 1⅓ cups.

RUSSIAN MAYONNAISE

- 4 tablespoons chili sauce
- 1 teaspoon chopped chives
- 2 tablespoons chopped pimiento
- 1 cup Basic Mayonnaise (at left)

In a small bowl combine chili sauce, chives, pimiento, and mayonnaise. Mix well and chill.

Makes 1¼ cups.

MAYONNAISE WITH NUTS

- 1 cup nuts, toasted and chopped (use any variety)
- 1 teaspoon Dijon mustard
- 1 cup Basic Mayonnaise (at left)

In a small bowl combine nuts, mustard, and mayonnaise; mix well.

Makes 2 cups.

MAYONNAISE NIÇOISE

- ½ cup tomato purée
- 1 small green bell pepper, chopped
- 1 cup Basic Mayonnaise (at left)
- 1 teaspoon chopped fresh tarragon
- 2 teaspoons chopped chives

In small pan cook tomato purée, stirring constantly, until most of the moisture has evaporated and the purée is very thick. Chill, then add to mayonnaise along with the pepper, tarragon, and chives.

Makes 1¼ cups.

TARTAR MAYONNAISE

- 1 cup Basic Mayonnaise (at left)
- 1 tablespoon finely chopped parsley
- 1 tablespoon chopped gherkin
- 1 tablespoon chopped green olives
- 1 tablespoon drained, chopped capers
- ½ teaspoon paprika

Combine mayonnaise, parsley, gherkin, olives, capers, and paprika; chill.

Makes about 1¼ cups.

DILL MAYONNAISE

½ cup finely chopped fresh dill
¼ cup grated onion
1 cup Basic Mayonnaise
(see page 117)

In a small bowl combine dill, onion, and mayonnaise; mix well.

Makes 1½ cups.

MUSTARD MAYONNAISE

2 teaspoons lemon juice
1 tablespoon Dijon mustard
1 cup Basic Mayonnaise
(see page 117)
⅓ cup whipping cream, beaten
into soft peaks
Dash hot-pepper sauce

In a small bowl combine lemon juice and mustard, mixing well. Add mixture to mayonnaise. Stir in beaten cream and hot-pepper sauce. Chill.

Makes 1½ cups.

BÉARNAISE MAYONNAISE

2 large shallots, peeled
and minced
½ cup white wine vinegar
3 tablespoons dried tarragon
½ teaspoon kosher salt
¼ teaspoon white pepper
1 teaspoon Dijon mustard
1½ cups Basic Mayonnaise
(see page 117)

In a small saucepan, bring shallots, vinegar, tarragon, salt, pepper, and mustard to a boil. Reduce mixture by one half. Let cool and add to mayonnaise.

Makes 1½ cups.

AÏOLI

3 to 6 cloves garlic
1 cup Basic Mayonnaise
(see page 117)

Pound garlic using a mortar and pestle. Mix with mayonnaise.

Makes 1 cup.

MAYONNAISE FINES HERBES

4 tablespoons chopped fresh
green herbs (such as parsley,
chives, tarragon, basil,
thyme, dill)
1 cup Basic Mayonnaise
(see page 117)

In a small bowl combine herbs with mayonnaise.

Makes 1 cup.

MAYONNAISE PERSILLADE

2 cloves garlic, finely minced
2 tablespoons chopped parsley
2 teaspoons Dijon mustard
½ teaspoon Worcestershire sauce
½ teaspoon white wine vinegar
Kosher salt and freshly
ground pepper to taste
1 cup Basic Mayonnaise
(see page 117)

In a small bowl mix garlic, parsley, mustard, Worcestershire, vinegar, salt, pepper, and mayonnaise.

Makes 1 cup.

RÉMOULADE

2 teaspoons finely
chopped capers
1 teaspoon chopped dill pickles
1 teaspoon Dijon mustard
1 chopped green onion (include
part of green)
1 cup Basic Mayonnaise
(see page 117)

In a small bowl mix capers, pickles, mustard, onion, and mayonnaise.

Makes 1 cup.

BASIC HOLLANDAISE SAUCE

3 tablespoons water
3 egg yolks
Salt and cayenne pepper
to taste
¾ cup unsalted butter at room
temperature, diced
1 tablespoon lemon juice, or
to taste

In a small pan over low heat or in double boiler, whisk water, yolks, salt, and cayenne for 30 seconds. Remove from heat, whisk in butter bit by bit. Return to heat if needed. Add lemon juice. Bottom of pan should never be hot to the touch or sauce will curdle. The sauce will be thick and creamy. Serve warm, not hot.

Makes 1 cup.

Maltaise Hollandaise Add ½ cup orange juice and 1 tablespoon grated orange rind to hollandaise; mix well.

Mireille Hollandaise Add 2 tablespoons tomato purée and 1 teaspoon minced fresh basil to hollandaise; mix well.

Chantilly Mousseline Hollandaise Add 2 tablespoons fish stock and 2 tablespoons stiffly beaten whipping cream to hollandaise.

Lemon Hollandaise Add 1 teaspoon freshly grated lemon peel and a pinch of cayenne pepper to hollandaise.

Curry Hollandaise Add 1 tablespoon curry powder to hollandaise.

Hollandaise Arlésienne Add 1 tablespoon anchovy paste to hollandaise.

FOOD PROCESSOR HOLLANDAISE SAUCE

4 egg yolks
2 tablespoons lemon juice
½ teaspoon salt
Dash hot-pepper sauce
½ cup unsalted butter, melted

In food processor fitted with steel blade, place egg yolks, lemon juice, salt, and hot-pepper sauce. Process for a few seconds. With the machine running, pour butter through the feed tube. The butter must be extremely hot and bubbling or the sauce will not thicken.

Makes about 1 cup.

BÉARNAISE SAUCE

¼ cup dry white wine
¼ cup wine vinegar
2 shallots, finely chopped
1 tablespoon chopped
fresh tarragon
3 egg yolks
Kosher salt and freshly
ground pepper
½ cup unsalted butter, diced

1. In a small saucepan boil wine, vinegar, shallots, and tarragon until a syrupy mixture remains. Cool slightly.

2. Over extremely low heat beat in egg yolks, salt, and pepper. The base of the pan should never be too hot to touch. When the mixture is creamy, whisk in butter bit by bit until a creamy emulsion has formed.

Makes 1 cup.

Food Processor Béarnaise Complete step 1 above. In a food processor fitted with steel blade, process egg yolks, salt, and pepper. Add slightly cooled tarragon mixture. With processor running, add butter bit by bit through the feed tube until a creamy emulsion has formed.

LEMON CRÈME FRAÎCHE

Buttermilk or sour cream may be used in place of the lemon juice to give a different flavor to the cream. Don't use the ultrapasteurized cream; it does not have the same flavor or consistency as plain pasteurized cream. Lemon Crème Fraîche will keep for weeks in the refrigerator.

1 cup whipping cream
2 tablespoons lemon juice

In a small bowl or a jar, mix whipping cream and lemon juice and let sit at room temperature until mixture thickens to the consistency of sour cream. This will take 12 to 24 hours depending on the temperature of the room. Refrigerate after thickening.

Makes 1 cup.

CRÈME FRAÎCHE SAUCE

½ pound yellow onions,
finely chopped
1 cup dry white wine
2 tablespoons lemon juice
Kosher salt and freshly
ground pepper
Cayenne pepper to taste
2 cups Lemon Crème Fraîche
(at left)

In a medium pan place onion, wine, and lemon juice. Cook until the liquid is reduced by one half and onion is soft. Add salt, pepper, cayenne, and Lemon Crème Fraîche; simmer 3 to 5 minutes.

Makes 2½ cups.

With wonderfully fresh spring asparagus and salmon, a rich, homemade hollandaise sauce adds your own gourmet touch. Preparation is easy and unhurried if you make the sauce ahead and keep it warm in a thermos.

Velouté Aurore

> 1 tablespoon tomato paste
> 1 egg yolk
>   Fish Velouté (at left)

Combine tomato paste, egg yolk, and velouté and mix well.

Velouté Bâtarde

> ¼ cup unsalted butter, softened
> 2 egg yolks
> ⅓ cup Fish Fumet (page 17)
> 1 tablespoon lemon juice
>   Fish Velouté (at left)

In a small bowl combine butter, yolks, fumet, and lemon juice. Mix well and add to velouté.

Caper Velouté

> 1 tablespoon capers, rinsed and drained
> 1 tablespoon white wine vinegar
>   Fish Velouté (at left)

Mix capers and vinegar with velouté.

Velouté Mornay

> 1 cup grated cheese
> ½ cup white wine
>   Fish Velouté (at left)

Mix cheese and wine with velouté.

Mustard Velouté

> 2 teaspoons Dijon mustard
>   Fish Velouté (at left)

Mix mustard with velouté.

Soubise Velouté

> ¼ cup unsalted butter
> 2 large onions, chopped
> 3 tablespoons dry white wine
>   Fish Velouté (at left)

In a small pan melt butter and sauté onions until soft. Add wine; cook for 2 to 3 minutes. Purée in processor. Add to velouté.

Few recipes establish a cook's reputation as well as a recipe for a flavorful sauce, but sauces need not be complicated. Hot sauces such as hollandaises and Fish Velouté must be served soon after preparation, but most other sauces can be prepared in advance and stored in the refrigerator until needed.

FISH VELOUTÉ

> 2 tablespoons unsalted butter
> 2 tablespoons flour
> 2 cups Fish Fumet (page 17)
>   Kosher salt and freshly ground white pepper

In a medium saucepan melt butter over low heat. Add flour and whisk continually for 2 to 3 minutes; do not brown. Pour fumet slowly into flour mixture (roux) and continue to whisk. Simmer over low heat, skimming occasionally to remove the skin of impurities that will form on the surface. Slow cooking is necessary to remove the taste of flour and to reduce sauce. When the mixture reaches the desired consistency, after 25 to 30 minutes, season to taste with salt and pepper.

Makes about 1¼ cups.

BENTLEY'S GARLIC SAUCE

Jo Policastro is the moving force behind Bentley's Restaurant in San Francisco. Well known for its outstanding fish and shellfish, the restaurant serves this garlic sauce, which is a wonderful accompaniment for fish recipes.

> 1 tablespoon chopped shallot
> 2 tablespoons chopped garlic
> 2 cups dry white wine
> ¼ cup garlic wine vinegar
> ½ cup whipping cream
> 1½ cups unsalted butter
> Salt and white pepper
> to taste

In a medium, heavy-bottomed pan, combine shallot, garlic, wine, and vinegar. Reduce over high heat to syrupy consistency. Add cream and bring to a boil. Reduce liquid by one third. Transfer to blender or food processor. With machine running, add butter bit by bit until smooth. Season to taste with salt and pepper.

Makes 1½ cups.

CUCUMBER YOGURT SAUCE

> ¾ cup peeled, seeded, minced cucumber
> 1 cup plain yogurt
> 1 tablespoon chopped fresh mint or ½ teaspoon dried
> ½ teaspoon finely minced garlic
> ½ teaspoon kosher salt
> ¼ teaspoon freshly ground white pepper

Sprinkle cucumber with salt and drain in colander for 30 minutes. In a medium bowl combine cucumber, yogurt, mint, garlic, salt, and pepper; mix well.

Makes 1½ cups.

CILANTRO CHUTNEY

To prepare a fresh coconut, puncture the dark "eyes" in the shell by hammering the tip of an ice pick through them. Drain the liquid. Bake the whole coconut in a preheated 350° F oven for 30 minutes. While still warm, hammer open the shell, which should separate from the meat. Pare brown skin off meat.

> ⅓ cup lemon juice
> 2 cups cilantro leaves
> ¼ cup peeled, chopped coconut
> ⅓ cup finely chopped green onion
> 1½ tablespoons minced fresh ginger
> 1 tablespoon seeded, chopped red or green chile pepper
> 2 teaspoons sugar
> 1 teaspoon ground cumin
> Kosher salt and freshly ground pepper to taste

Place lemon juice and half the cilantro in a food processor fitted with steel blade; purée. Add remaining cilantro, coconut, onion, ginger, chile pepper, sugar, and cumin; process until smooth. Taste and season with salt and pepper. Serve as soon as possible.

Makes 2 cups.

CUMBERLAND SAUCE

> 2 large shallots, minced
> ⅓ cup red currant jelly
> ⅓ cup orange juice
> ⅓ cup tawny port
> 3 tablespoons lemon juice
> 2 teaspoons cornstarch
> 1 tablespoon cold water

In a small saucepan combine shallots, jelly, orange juice, and port. Simmer for 10 minutes, then add lemon juice. In a small bowl dissolve cornstarch in water, then whisk the mixture into the hot sauce. Continue to whisk until the sauce is thick. Let cool and serve chilled.

Makes about 1 cup.

PROSCIUTTO SALSA

> 2 tablespoons olive oil
> 1 small onion, minced
> 1 tablespoon minced capers
> 6 ounces prosciutto, cut in thick slices, then minced
> 2 teaspoons minced fresh basil
> 2 teaspoons minced parsley
> 2 tablespoons Fish Fumet (page 17)
> 2 tablespoons lemon juice
> 4 anchovy fillets, minced
> Freshly ground black pepper to taste

In a medium sauté pan heat olive oil. Add onion, capers, and prosciutto; cook until onions are soft and prosciutto begins to brown. Add basil, parsley, and fumet. Remove from heat and add lemon juice and anchovies, mixing well. Season with pepper.

Makes 1½ cups.

ONION SAUCE

> ¼ cup unsalted butter
> 2 large onions, thinly sliced
> 3 tablespoons flour
> 1¼ cups Fish Fumet (page 17)
> 1 teaspoon dried tarragon
> 2 teaspoons balsamic vinegar
> Kosher salt and freshly ground pepper to taste
> Dash hot-pepper sauce

In a medium sauté pan, melt butter. Add onions and cook until soft and golden. Sprinkle flour over onion and mix well. Add fumet slowly and stir until thick. Add tarragon and vinegar, mixing well. Season to taste with salt, pepper, and hot-pepper sauce.

Makes about 3 cups.

121

TOMATO SAUCE

- 1 tablespoon olive oil
- 1 large onion, chopped
- 8 medium tomatoes, chopped
- 1 garlic clove, minced
- 1 tablespoon chopped parsley
- 1 teaspoon dried thyme
  Kosher salt and freshly ground pepper to taste

In a large pan heat oil and sauté onion until soft. Add tomatoes, garlic, parsley, thyme, salt, and pepper. Simmer gently until the mixture has been reduced to a thick pulp. Sieve the mixture. If it is too watery, place over medium heat and reduce to desired consistency.

Makes about 1 cup.

ASPIC

- 3 cups Fish Fumet (page 17)
- 1 egg white, beaten
- 1 eggshell, finely crushed
- 2 envelopes (2 tablespoons) unflavored gelatin
- 2 tablespoons dry sherry

Strain fumet through dampened cheesecloth into a medium bowl. Refrigerate fumet for several hours to allow the fine particles to form a sediment. Pour off clear liquid. To clarify, transfer fumet to a medium saucepan and add beaten egg white and crushed eggshell. Over high heat whisk rapidly. Egg white will form a curdlike layer. Remove from heat and let stand 5 minutes. Strain through dampened cheesecloth into bowl. Meanwhile soften gelatin in sherry (3 to 5 minutes). Add to strained fumet and cool to room temperature.

Makes 3 cups.

COCKTAIL SAUCE

- ¾ cup tomato-based chili sauce
- 1 to 3 teaspoons prepared horseradish
- 1 teaspoon Worcestershire sauce
- 1 small clove garlic, minced
- 2 teaspoons lemon juice
  Kosher salt and freshly ground pepper to taste
- 1 tablespoon finely minced celery

In a small bowl combine chili sauce, horseradish, Worcestershire, garlic, lemon juice, salt, pepper, and celery. Mix well and chill.

Makes about 1 cup.

CAPER SAUCE

- 1 cup Basic Mayonnaise (see page 117)
- 2 teaspoons capers, drained and chopped
- 1 fresh gherkin, chopped
- 1 teaspoon chopped fresh fennel
- 1 teaspoon chopped chives
- 1 tablespoon Dijon mustard
- 1 tablespoon minced parsley

Combine mayonnaise, capers, gherkin, fennel, chives, mustard, and parsley; chill.

Makes 1¼ cups.

TAHINI WALNUT SAUCE

- 1 cup walnuts
- 2 cloves garlic
- 6 tablespoons tahini
- 3 tablespoons lemon juice
- ¼ cup chopped parsley
- 1 tablespoon water
  Kosher salt and freshly ground pepper to taste

In a food processor fitted with steel blade, combine walnuts, garlic, tahini, lemon juice, parsley, water, salt, and pepper until blended. Don't overprocess; the walnuts should add a bit of texture to the sauce.

Makes 1½ to 2 cups.

SKORDALIA

A classic Greek sauce—delicious with any fish or shellfish.

- 3 slices firm white bread, crusts removed
- 6 large cloves garlic
- 2 egg yolks
- ¼ cup blanched almonds
- 1½ tablespoons lemon juice
- ½ to ¾ cup olive oil
- 2 tablespoons chopped parsley

Soak bread in cold water, squeeze dry. In food processor fitted with steel blade, process bread, garlic, egg yolks, almonds, and lemon juice until evenly chopped. With the machine running, pour olive oil through the feed tube. The consistency should be that of thick mayonnaise. Add parsley and process to distribute evenly.

Makes 1 cup.

HORSERADISH CRÈME WITH NUTS

Serve this sauce with cold poached fish or grilled seafood.

- ½ cup Lemon Crème Fraîche (see page 119) or sour cream
- 2 tablespoons prepared white horseradish
- 1 tablespoon Champagne white wine vinegar
- 2 teaspoons Dijon mustard
- ½ teaspoon sugar
- ½ cup whipping cream, beaten into soft peaks
- ⅓ cup finely chopped pecans, roasted

Combine Lemon Crème Fraîche, horseradish, vinegar, mustard, and sugar. Fold in cream and pecans.

Makes 1½ cups.

The number of possible combinations is almost infinite when fish and shellfish are combined with different sauces, herbs, spices, and vegetables.

INDEX

127

U.S. MEASURE AND METRIC MEASURE CONVERSION CHART

Formulas for Exact Measures

Rounded Measures for Quick Reference

Mass (Weight)

Symbol	When you know:	Multiply by:	To find:			
oz	ounces	28.35	grams	1 oz		= 30 g
lb	pounds	0.45	kilograms	4 oz		= 115 g
g	grams	0.035	ounces	8 oz		= 225 g
kg	kilograms	2.2	pounds	16 oz	= 1 lb	= 450 g
				32 oz	= 2 lb	= 900 g
				36 oz	= 2¼ lb	= 1,000 g (1 kg)

Volume

Symbol	When you know:	Multiply by:	To find:			
tsp	teaspoons	5.0	milliliters	¼ tsp	= ¹⁄₂₄ oz	= 1 ml
tbsp	tablespoons	15.0	milliliters	½ tsp	= ¹⁄₁₂ oz	= 2 ml
fl oz	fluid ounces	29.57	milliliters	1 tsp	= ⅙ oz	= 5 ml
c	cups	0.24	liters	1 tbsp	= ½ oz	= 15 ml
pt	pints	0.47	liters	1 c	= 8 oz	= 250 ml
qt	quarts	0.95	liters	2 c (1 pt)	= 16 oz	= 500 ml
gal	gallons	3.785	liters	4 c (1 qt)	= 32 oz	= 1 l.
ml	milliliters	0.034	fluid ounces	4 qt (1 gal)	= 128 oz	= 3¾ l.

Length

Symbol	When you know:	Multiply by:	To find:		
in.	inches	2.54	centimeters	⅜ in.	= 1 cm
ft	feet	30.48	centimeters	1 in.	= 2.5 cm
yd	yards	0.9144	meters	2 in.	= 5 cm
mi	miles	1.609	kilometers	2½ in.	= 6.5 cm
km	kilometers	0.621	miles	12 in. (1 ft)	= 30 cm
m	meters	1.094	yards	1 yd	= 90 cm
cm	centimeters	0.39	inches	100 ft	= 30 m
				1 mi	= 1.6 km

Temperature

Symbol	When you know:	Multiply by:	To find:		
° F	Fahrenheit	5/9 (after subtracting 32)	Celsius	32° F	= 0° C
° C	Celsius	9/5 (then add 32)	Fahrenheit	68° F	= 20° C
				212° F	= 100° C

Area

Symbol	When you know:	Multiply by:	To find:		
in.²	square inches	6.452	square centimeters	1 in.²	= 6.5 cm²
ft²	square feet	929.0	square centimeters	1 ft²	= 930 cm²
yd²	square yards	8,361.0	square centimeters	1 yd²	= 8,360 cm²
a	acres	0.4047	hectares	1 a	= 4,050 m²